TASTY™

total comfort

TASTY™

total comfort

COZY RECIPES WITH A MODERN TOUCH

Clarkson Potter/Publishers
NEW YORK

Contents

Introduction

Just like putting on an old sweater or pressing Play to watch a favorite movie, a good meal has the power to comfort us. When that meal has all the familiarity of home, family, and love, the comfort can be next-level powerful.

Welcome to *Tasty Total Comfort*, a book stuffed to the brim with 75 timeless and super-satisfying recipes—everything from hearty breakfasts, satisfying lunches, cozy dinners, exciting sides, classic desserts, and refreshing drinks that will quickly become your go-to, gotta-have, how-did-I-live-without, I-could-do-this-in-my-sleep recipes.

Just like every culture has unique, quirky, and maybe slightly embarrassing traditions, these recipes reflect everything that makes American comfort food so special. The United States is unique in its blend of broad ideas, perspectives, cultures, origins, and experiences. Our food can't help but reflect that blending because what we consider American cuisine is, at its foundation, a crossroads of immigration. Traditional dishes from across Africa, Asia, Europe, and South America, intermingled with those of our own indigenous populations to create the backbone of the American diet. Over time, those cuisines morphed into something slightly different, special, and uniquely American. But it all came from somewhere, and the story behind that journey is what makes it valuable.

But, hey, cooking is fun and so is this book! While we respect traditions, we also fully believe that modern perspectives and creative twists are always welcome. The recipes in this book build on flavors and techniques you already know and love, but they add something new to the conversation. Dishes like Huevos Rancheros Breakfast Tostadas (page 44), Fried Chicken Adobo (page 63), Spaghetti-Ohs alla Vodka (page 76), Eggplant Parm Casserole (page 84), Aloo Gobi Soup (page 97), or Senegalese Sombi pudding cups (page 139) present home-cooked favorites in a whole new light. Pigs in a Blanket Pull-Apart Bread (page 132) brings the classic snack to new heights (literally), while Jamaican Jerk Pulled-Pork Sandwich (page 89) marries all the complex flavors of jerk with the portable convenience of a bun. Gravy-Stuffed Cheddar Biscuit Bombs (page 31) is the biscuits-and-gravy upgrade you didn't know you needed, and Chocolate Halva Truffles (page 161) make the classic dessert dangerously easy to keep eating.

Of course, we also include the familiar comfort staples of American food, streamlined with the modern home cook in mind. Favorites like Matzo Ball Soup (page 55), Shrimp Pad Thai (page 105), Ghanaian Jollof Rice (page 125), Sheet Pan Strawberry French Toast (page 36), Loco Moco (page 43), Chicken Fried Steak & Gravy (page 60), Eid Cookies (page 157), Haitian Macaroni au Gratin (page 67), Ginger Congee with Eggs & Scallion Oil (page 47), and Tater Tot Hotdish (page 94) are all here and ready for you to make them right now! We also grabbed some lesser-known favorites like Egyptian Pumpkin Pie (page 153), a perfectly spiced (and crustless!) pie that deserves a prime spot on every Thanksgiving table, or Korean Hot Dogs (page 59), a wildly creative riff on American corn dogs. Grape Jelly Meatballs (page 93) are far more delicious than they sound (just trust us on this one), and Agua Fresca with Chia (page 180) is undoubtedly the most satisfying thing you'll drink all year.

We hope the food in this book will bring that nostalgic feeling of cozy satisfaction. In times of need or celebration, whether you're gathered with family or friends or are dining solo, we hope these dishes fill your home with all the warm smells and cheerful sounds of classic home cooking. But most of all, we hope you'll find yourself reaching for these recipes again and again—until they become your own version of total comfort.

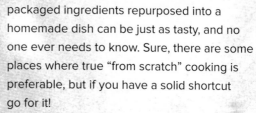

How to Use This Book

Every home cook knows two things:

1 Recipes are living documents.

2 If you find a shortcut, take it.

We firmly believe that "made from scratch" means you took the time to make it yourself, put love and care into the preparation, and left your mark on the presentation. Beyond that, we firmly believe in cooking smarter, not harder. There's no shame in leaning on store-bought ingredients when that saves you time, money, sanity, or all of the above. Common

packaged ingredients repurposed into a homemade dish can be just as tasty, and no one ever needs to know. Sure, there are some places where true "from scratch" cooking is preferable, but if you have a solid shortcut go for it!

As for the recipes, sit down: we need to have a talk. Not to shatter the illusion here, but Grandma didn't invent all her go-to recipes. She likely pulled many of them from an old cookbook, magazine, or newspaper, or she learned them from someone who got them from a cookbook, magazine—you get the point. But those recipes, over time, developed and changed, were written and rewritten on scraps of paper, and were adapted and substituted until they became hers.

Think of this book as the entry point for your own set of specialty recipes. These 75 recipes are tried and true, tested to perfection and meticulously edited. But they're *your* recipes now. Go ahead and fill the book with scribbled notes, adjust the seasonings to your taste, add your secrets in the margins, and play with them until they feel unique to you. That's how you start the journey from delicious dishes to total comfort.

The Modern American Pantry

This book uses a range of ingredients; some you might already have, some you might need to go looking for. But everything called for in this book should be readily available in most major grocery stores, and that might even encourage you to see familiar aisles in a new light. (We'll note the few things that might require specialty or online shopping.) Welcome to your modern American pantry!

Fats

Extra-virgin olive oil. There are some delicious and inexpensive brands of extra-virgin olive oil in every grocery store, perfect for everyday cooking. Keeping a second bottle of more expensive, super-flavorful EVOO for dressings, dips, and finishing dishes is a pro move.

Neutral oil. With light flavors and high smoke points, neutral oils are perfect for deep-frying, stir-frying, and high-intensity cooking. Vegetable, canola, and grapeseed oils are all affordable, versatile choices.

Sesame oil. Look for a reasonably priced bottle of pure sesame oil. Toasted sesame oil is great for sauces and finishing dishes but will become bitter at high heat.

Nonstick cooking spray. A can of neutral oil is best; skip the butter or flour varieties, which can burn quickly.

Unsalted butter. Stick with unsalted so you can control the salt levels in your food. We think good butter is worth its weight in gold.

Acids

Red wine vinegar. Super-flavorful red wine vinegar adds a lot of punch to any dish. Use it to stand up to (or cut through) big, rich flavors.

White wine vinegar. Good for dressing delicate salads or lighter meats.

Rice vinegar. Has a subtle sweetness that is the go-to in East Asian cooking. Look for unseasoned.

Cider vinegar. An unmistakable sweet-tart flavor that is a perfect accent for a wide variety of dishes.

Coconut vinegar. Already a staple in Southeast Asia and parts of India, the light sweetness and mild acidity make for a very versatile vinegar.

Condiments

Dijon mustard. Forget all other mustards—this is the one. Dressings, sauces, and sandwiches will get a ton of flavor, without an overpowering aftertaste.

Yellow mustard. Okay, we take it back. Yellow mustard is the classic for a reason and it's always there when you do need a strong mustard-y flavor.

Mayonnaise. Mayo is a secret weapon for adding a ton of flavor and holding everything together.

Ketchup. Not just for burgers, ketchup is great for adding savory acidity to sauces and glazes.

Hot sauce. Hot sauces can range from Mexican style to the ubiquitous sriracha. Pick one that you love for everyday use and grab a couple other styles to meet the needs of specific dishes. (But let's be honest; if you're a Hot Sauce Person, you already have at least six in the fridge.)

Tamari and soy sauce. Tamari is a Japanese variation on Chinese soy sauce. It's a little more savory than the salty punch of the Chinese, and is often gluten-free (check the label to be sure), but both can be used fairly interchangeably.

Fish sauce. Fish sauce is an Asian miracle product that is not fishy, but somehow sweet, salty, and savory all at the same time. Tamari, soy sauce, or Worcestershire sauce can substitute in an emergency, but nothing can replicate the unique flavor of fish sauce.

Worcestershire sauce. Say it with us, WOO-stah-shur. The impossible-to-pronounce but necessary-to-use sauce adds a deep savory kick. There are anchovies in the sauce, so look for a vegetarian version if you need one.

Honey. Honey can be expensive, but it's worth it to invest in a good bottle, preferably one that's from somewhere local.

Pure maple syrup. Similar to honey, real maple syrup can be pricey. But the fake stuff (which is just flavored corn syrup) can't come close to the real thing.

Cans, Jars, and Boxes

Salsa. A jar of chunky salsa is useful for more than just chips. It's a great addition to soups, bean salads, and breakfast scrambles. Keep a couple jars on hand at all times.

Tamarind paste. One of the main ingredients in pad Thai, tamarind paste is a nice balance of sweet and sour. Most grocery stores should have a jar, but you can always find it at a specialty Asian market or order it online in a pinch.

Stock. Chicken, beef, and vegetable stock (or broth; the terms are generally used interchangeably in packaging) are the building blocks of savory cooking. We prefer to avoid low-sodium stocks because they tend to suck the life out of a dish.

Canned beans. Canned beans are one of the few products where canned is equally good as homemade. (And a real time-saver.) We use black, kidney, chickpeas, and cannellini beans in this book, which always benefit from draining and rinsing.

Canned tomatoes. Ripe, fresh tomatoes are always better, but canned are often more reliable. (And, again, a real time-saver.) Double-check the label before buying because the differences among crushed, diced, and whole are pretty significant.

Tomato paste. Often sold in a can or a squeeze tube. The can is great if you're using it all at once, the tube is best if you're planning to use a tablespoon at a time.

Canned milks. Usually stacked together in the grocery store are evaporated milk, sweetened condensed milk, cream of coconut, and full-fat coconut milk. All are delicious, but they are not interchangeable. Make sure you grab the right one because they have different fat and sugar contents that could really derail your dish.

Dried Goods

Pasta. Pasta comes in all shapes, sizes, and textures. In this book we use the standard Italian shapes, like spaghetti, elbow, and rigatoni, but we also use the ring-shaped anellini, which might need to be sourced online. We also use egg noodles and rice noodles, both of which can easily be found in most grocery stores.

Rice. Rice is the great global connector, since almost every country uses it as a dietary staple. Keep a couple varieties of rice, like short-grain and long-grain, on hand at all times.

Chia. A powerhouse of nutrients and protein, chia seeds are great to have around. Look for this near the rice and other grains.

Grits. Grits are ground dried corn bits, and they come in several varieties, like stone-ground, quick-cooking, and instant. Quick grits are the perfect mix of shelf stable and controlled cooking, so they're our go-to.

Bread crumbs. Perfect for binding, coating, and topping, bread crumbs are the triple threat worth keeping around. Buy plain crumbs; you can add spices as needed.

Panko. Panko are dryer and flakier crumbs than regular bread crumbs and they absorb less oil for lighter and crunchier fried food.

Flour. All-purpose is the standard for most recipes. Any whole wheat, nut, or cereal flours should be stored in the refrigerator or freezer because they contain high levels of natural oils and will spoil at room temperature.

Matzo meal. Matzo meal is made by grinding matzo, or unleavened flatbread. While primarily used to make matzo balls or in baking, matzo meal can also substitute for bread crumbs in most cases.

Yeast. Yeast is the powerhouse for rising bread dough. You'll usually see two types of yeast: active dry or instant rise (sometimes labeled as quick rise or rapid rise). We prefer active dry yeast, which first needs to blooms in warm water, offering the security of knowing the yeast is still good. Instant yeast gets mixed directly into the dough and you won't know until the end if it activated or not. All yeast should be stored in the freezer for extended shelf life and maximum effectiveness.

Baking soda and baking powder. Both are leavening agents, but they react differently. Baking soda reacts to acid, so the rise begins immediately. Baking powder reacts to acid and heat, so the reaction starts immediately, but the rise happens in the oven. Note that the two agents cannot be used interchangeably, even though they're often used together.

Cornstarch. Perfect for thickening soups, sauces, and desserts with no detectable taste, cornstarch is a pantry must-have.

Granulated sugar. The building block for most dessert recipes, this is the standard white sugar you see everywhere. It adds a perfect neutral sweetness.

Light brown sugar. Brown sugar is granulated sugar mixed with molasses. Light brown sugar has a subtle flavor, giving it a high adaptability for desserts or adding a sweet note to savory dishes. Store tightly wrapped or in an airtight container to prevent drying out.

Dark brown sugar. With its higher molasses content and stronger flavor than light brown sugar, we use dark brown sugar when we need assertively rich flavors. Store tightly wrapped or in an airtight container to prevent drying out.

Powdered sugar. Powdered sugar (sometimes labeled as 10X, icing, or confectioners' sugar) is the perfect finishing touch to a homemade dish and is essential for glazes and frostings.

Cocoa powder. Because cocoa powder has no sugar, it can easily transition between sweet and savory. Cocoa powder is slightly acidic, so it adds a nice balance to rich or spicy dishes like stews or chilis, and also gives an airy rise to cakes and cookies. You'll see products labeled Dutch-processed or natural. We prefer natural for its easier price point and sharper flavor, but they are generally interchangeable in recipes.

Instant coffee. Besides being the fast track to a morning cup, instant coffee is a secret weapon for making chocolate desserts taste more chocolate-y. (You'll never taste it, we swear.)

Taro powder. Used to make bubble tea, but also handy for sweetening desserts or adding a vibrant purple color to frosting, taro powder might require a trip to the Asian market or a few clicks online. Look for an unsweetened powder so you can control the sugar.

Boba. The "bubble" in bubble tea, boba are tapioca pearls, made from tapioca starch, and they are typically sold dried. We prefer the black tapioca pearls for their chewiness, adaptability, and accessibility. Your local Asian market will probably have them, or they're easily sourced online.

Nuts. Nuts like almonds, walnuts, pecans, and pistachios all have high oil contents and should be stored in the freezer to prevent spoilage. Just remember to bring them to room temperature before toasting.

Dairy

Milk. We rely on whole milk throughout this book because the fat content makes everything the smoothest, creamiest, and richest version of itself. Percentage (1% or 2%), skim, and plant-based milks can be swapped in as needed.

Buttermilk. A staple of American cooking and baking, buttermilk is slightly acidic, like yogurt, to give desserts a puffy rise or cut through rich savory flavors. (Speaking of yogurt, it can be used in place of buttermilk in most cases.)

Sour cream. Another acidic staple, sour cream has a thicker texture and is perfect for the finishing touch or a thick and creamy sauce. Just like buttermilk, yogurt can substitute in most cases.

Cream cheese. We prefer cream cheese in the blocks, rather than the tubs, for easy access. Whipped cream cheese is great for bagels, but not helpful for cooking.

Shredded cheese. Packaged shredded cheese can be frozen and thawed later, so buy in bulk if you have the option. And just remember; shredded cheese is coated with powders to ensure its shreds don't stick together, so freshly shredded cheese will always give you a better melt.

Feta. Fresh feta cheese in blocks will have a smoother texture than crumbled feta. (Similar to shredded cheese, it's commercially formulated not to clump.)

Cotija. Cotija is usually sold in circular containers in the cheese section, sometimes wrapped in a banana leaf. If you can't find cotija, feta is a good substitute.

Seasonings

Salt. Kosher salt should be your standard—and Diamond Crystal is our recommended brand. It's flaky enough to pinch and season with ease, but it isn't as aggressively salty as other types. (Plus, it's cheap in bulk!) Also invest in a good flaky sea salt, like Maldon or Jacobsen, for finishing touches on desserts, meats, and vegetables.

Black pepper. Buy a sturdy pepper grinder and restock the peppercorns as needed. Nothing beats freshly ground black pepper—the oils in the peppercorns activate for an extra pepper-y taste, plus you can control the grind from fine to coarse.

Bay leaves. They're the invisible ingredient because you won't be able to pinpoint their flavor, but you'll be missing something if they're not there. Fresh bay leaves have a slightly different (and stronger) flavor than dried, so use about half the amount if substituting fresh.

Dried herbs and spices. Dried herbs are generally much more powerful than fresh, so reduce by a third if subbing in dried. Dried spices in general are best when heat and fat can activate the flavor (known as blooming), so make sure they interact with heat at some point while using them. And store them in a dark and cool place to keep their flavors fresh longer.

Sesame seeds. Sesame seeds (like most nuts and seeds) have a high oil content, so store them in the fridge or freezer for maximum shelf life. They're best when freshly toasted in a dry skillet over low heat.

Sazón. There are a few varieties of Sazón, a spice blend usually sold in packets and small containers. We particularly love the coriander and annatto flavors for the vibrant color and savory punch, but they're all delicious.

Nutritional yeast. Sometimes it's sold with the baking yeast, sometimes it's found in the spice aisle. But a few shakes of these golden flakes and you'll be hooked. They have a similar umami flavor to cheese, so they're perfect for vegan cooking, sprinkled over pasta, and even topping popcorn.

Other Staples

Wine. A good bottle of wine gives dishes a sweet acidity that can't be replicated. Buy something that's on the cheaper side but would still be delicious to sip while you cook.

White miso. The most mild of the miso family, white miso adds rich umami flavor that's hard to beat. Look for it in the refrigerated area.

Flour and corn tortillas. Both delicious, but very different from each other. Flour tortillas are soft and pliable, which means they won't hold up very long against sauce-heavy dishes. Corn tortillas are studier bases and can even be fried for crispy tostadas or homemade tortilla chips. Store them both in the fridge for longer shelf life.

Meats, produce, herbs, and dairy should be purchased as close as possible to the day you'll need them. Buying meat in bulk can be cheaper in the long run, so portion and freeze what you don't immediately need. Just remember to move it to the refrigerator at least twelve hours before you need it, so it has time to defrost.

Buying vegetables and herbs in small quantities may seem tedious, but it's cheaper than throwing them out after a few days. Some frozen vegetables, like peas, corn, and carrots, are often tastier and easier to use than buying fresh. (We rely on frozen a lot in this book!) Similarly, frozen fruit can be useful in months when fresh is out of season.

The Family Kitchen

The Starter Pack

Let's start with the basics. Shop around (or read reviews!) to find the intersection of cheap but well-made tools. Every kitchen should have:

Measuring spoons. Preferably ranging from ¼ teaspoon to 1 tablespoon.

Measuring cups. Cups for measuring dry items ranging from ¼ cup to 1 cup and cups for measuring liquids that go to 2 cups.

Cutting board. Go big, sturdy, and nonslip. Don't worry about having separate ones for meat, fish, and vegetables; just wash your cutting board well between uses.

Fine-mesh strainer. Get a large one for draining pasta, rinsing beans, and sprinkling powdered sugar. The uses are endless.

Chef's knife. This is practically the only knife you need. It doesn't have to be expensive; just make sure it's a comfortable size and weight for you—you'll be using it a lot. A dull knife puts you in danger of slippage and accidents, so also invest in a knife sharpener to keep it in prime shape (or find out where you can have it sharpened).

Paring knife. This is much smaller than a chef's knife, ideal for precise tasks, like trimming or making small slices.

Serrated knife. Available in multiple sizes, serrated knives are handy for tricky work like cutting bread, slicing tomatoes, halving sandwiches, and peeling tough fruits like pineapple.

Wooden spoon. Gentle enough to stir, sturdy enough to smash.

Rubber spatula. Perfect for mixing, folding, scraping, and dividing.

Whisk. One large classic whisk will do everything you need it to.

Silicone tongs. Silicone tips are better than metal for a no-slip grip, plus they won't scratch cookware. Great for everything from flipping meat to lifting cooked spaghetti out of the water, to rescuing a stray potato. (Switch back to metal for high-heat tasks like grilling!)

Can opener. The classic manual one still works best and doesn't take up counter space.

Ladle. Great for soups, obviously, but also perfect for dividing batter, making pancakes, and drizzling sauces on dishes.

Rolling pin. Roll out dough, crush ice, and make crumbs out of graham crackers. A single cylinder of wood makes for the handiest and most versatile type of roller.

Microplane grater. Zest citrus, finely grate cheese, process ginger and garlic, grind nutmeg.

Vegetable peeler. Peel apples and potatoes, grate big pieces of Parmesan, shave chocolate garnishes. Y-shaped or swivel work about the same, so it's up to you.

Bowls. Find a stackable set of small, medium, and large bowls for easy storage. Stainless steel is the best for easy cleaning and won't hold odors like plastic can.

Oven mitts and trivet. Find a comfortable set of oven mitts and a trivet for hot pots and pans.

Kitchen towels. Decorative tea towels are wonderful. But kitchen towels (more absorbent and eco-friendly than paper towels) are the best for catching spills and cleaning up surfaces. In a pinch, you can use these on a hot surface as well.

Food storage. For packing lunches, storing leftovers, freezing soups. Glass or silicone sets are great, but a cheap, reliable, and eco-friendly move is washing and saving takeout containers. (The round quart-size containers are storage gold.)

Plastic wrap, aluminum foil, and parchment paper. For all things storage and baking.

Ruler. Keep a 24-inch metal ruler for kitchen-use only. Essential for measuring pastry, but also handy for rolling up dough.

Rimmed baking sheet. Find a half-size sheet pan that's roughly 18 by 13 inches with a 1-inch rim. Go for a thick, sturdy pan that will hold its shape and evenly conduct heat for perfect browning every time.

Large and small saucepans. For basics, from making rice to reheating leftovers.

Nonstick skillet. Great for scrambled eggs, pancakes, and anything delicate that shouldn't be heavily seared.

Cast-iron skillet. For getting a hard sear on meats and vegetables and for moving back and forth between the stove and oven. Investing in a good 12-inch skillet (and taking care of it; see note, following) will take your cooking over the top.

    Note: Cleaning a cast-iron skillet is the most important part of owning one. Use warm water and a pan brush to get the surface clean. Use a mixture of kosher salt and a few drops of oil to scrub off any stuck-on bits. Soap can be your absolute last resort, but never use any abrasive sponges. Place the skillet on a burner over high heat to dry it thoroughly. Remove it from the heat, dab a paper towel with vegetable oil, and wipe the entire inside of the skillet to coat. Allow it to cool completely before storing.

Blender and food processor. Plenty of brands make great multi-use blenders with food processor attachments. Save space (and money!) by getting a ninja-like machine that can do both.

9 by 13-inch metal baking pan. For making rolls, bars, and other treats.

8-inch square baking pan. Great for making desserts on a slightly smaller scale.

Level Up

Most of these are more *wants* than needs, but if you're cooking everyday these will quickly become more *needs* than wants.

Masking tape and permanent marker. Anything that goes in your fridge or freezer should be labeled with a name and date. (You might want to add your initials, too, in roommate situations.)

Fish spatula. Thinner and sleeker than a standard spatula, the fish spatula can sneak into tight places while still flipping everything from meat to pancakes.

Spider skimmer. Think of this as a slotted spoon, but more efficient. It'll immediately become your essential for frying foods.

Electric hand mixer. A whisk can do everything a hand mixer can do, but it sure is easier when you can give your arm a break.

Stand mixer. The boss level of mixing equipment. Make frosting, dough, batter, whipped cream, and even shred chicken with almost no effort.

Cake pans. Cake pans are kind of a single-use item. (Spoiler: It's cake.) Recipes can call for a variety of diameters and heights, so these are items that you'll likely accumulate over time as needed.

Tart pan. More shallow than a cake pan, with a removable bottom and crinkled edges, tart pans are perfect for making tarts (obviously), but also great for quiche and can even double as a pie plate.

Bundt pan. Available in endless fun shapes, with just as many fun uses, a Bundt pan is a great secret weapon in the kitchen.

Dutch oven. This large, heavy pot can be a little pricey, but it's worth the investment. Use it to make soups, boil pasta, and deep-fry. A 6-quart capacity one will be just right.

Instant-read thermometer. Buy a digital one for quick reads on cooking meat temperatures and to check if your oil is ready for frying.

Pizza cutter. True, a knife can do the job. But this multipurpose tool glides through sandwiches, quesadillas, raw dough, and more.

Cookie scoops. Usually sold in a set with varying sizes, these scoops are perfect for portioning dough, batter, frosting, and tons of other uses.

Kitchen torch. A true splurge, but the flame lends picture-perfect browning to desserts, bread crumbs, melted cheese, and marshmallows.

The Most Important Meal

CLASSIC DINER OMELETS each makes 1 omelet

Omelets are believed to have originated in ancient Persia, in a form very similar to the herb-packed Iranian kuku. So many cultures have a riff on the omelet, like the Filipino torta, the Italian frittata, the Spanish tortilla, or the Japanese tamagoyaki. But for the style we know and love—fluffy, gooey, and folded—we owe a big merci to France. Here are four of our absolute favorite omelets, all as classically American as a roadside diner.

Denver Omelet

3 **large eggs**

¼ teaspoon **kosher salt**

¼ teaspoon **freshly ground black pepper**

1 tablespoon **unsalted butter**

¼ cup **cubed ham**

¼ cup diced **green bell pepper**

¼ cup diced **red onion**

¼ cup **shredded Colby jack cheese**

1 **scallion**, white and green parts thinly sliced

1 In a medium bowl, whisk together the eggs, salt, and pepper.

2 Melt the butter in a medium nonstick skillet over medium heat. Add the ham, bell pepper, and red onion. Cook, stirring occasionally, until the onion and pepper are soft and the ham is warmed through, about 5 minutes. Spoon the filling into a small bowl, leaving the remaining butter in the skillet.

3 Pour the eggs into the skillet, swirling to create an even layer. Cover the skillet and cook the omelet undisturbed for about 5 minutes, until set. Distribute the cooked filling over the omelet along with the cheese. Use a spatula to fold the omelet in half and slide it onto a plate. Sprinkle the scallion over the top and serve immediately.

Four Cheese Omelet

3 **large eggs**

¼ teaspoon **kosher salt**

¼ teaspoon **freshly ground black pepper**

1 tablespoon **unsalted butter**

1 cup total of four different **shredded cheeses**, such as **cheddar**, **Asiago**, **Monterey jack**, **mozzarella**, **provolone**, or **Colby**

Chopped **fresh chives**, for serving

1 In a medium bowl, whisk together the eggs, salt, and pepper.

2 In a medium nonstick skillet, melt the butter over medium heat. Pour the eggs into the skillet, swirling to create an even layer. Cover the skillet and cook the omelet undisturbed for about 3 minutes, until almost set. Distribute the cheeses over the omelet and cover the skillet. Cook for about 2 minutes more, until the cheeses are melted. Use a spatula to fold the omelet in half and slide it onto a plate. Sprinkle the chives over the top and serve immediately.

Mediterranean Omelet

3 large eggs

¼ teaspoon **kosher salt**

¼ teaspoon **freshly ground black pepper**

1 tablespoon **unsalted butter**

1 cup **fresh spinach**, roughly chopped

¼ cup **sliced black olives**

¼ cup diced **ripe tomato**

¼ cup **crumbled feta cheese**

Chopped **fresh parsley**, for serving

1 In a medium bowl, whisk together the eggs, salt, and pepper.

2 In a medium nonstick skillet, melt the butter over medium heat. Pour the eggs into the skillet, swirling to create an even layer. Cover the skillet and cook the omelet undisturbed for about 5 minutes, until set. Distribute the spinach, olives, tomato, and feta over the omelet. Use a spatula to fold the omelet in half and slide it onto a plate. Sprinkle the parsley over the top and serve immediately.

L.E.O. Omelet

3 large eggs

¼ teaspoon **kosher salt**

¼ teaspoon **freshly ground black pepper**

1 tablespoon **unsalted butter**

4 ounces thin-sliced **lox**

¼ cup sliced **red onion**

1 tablespoon drained **capers**

1 tablespoon **fresh dill fronds**

1 In a medium bowl, whisk together the eggs, salt, and pepper.

2 In a medium nonstick skillet, melt the butter over medium heat. Pour the eggs into the skillet, swirling to create an even layer. Cover the skillet and cook the omelet undisturbed for about 5 minutes, until set. Distribute the lox, red onion, capers, and half the dill over the omelet. Use a spatula to fold the omelet in half and slide it onto a plate. Sprinkle the remaining dill over the top and serve immediately.

Helpful Hint

Many recipes call for a splash of milk, but we say to save it for the coffee mug. Adding milk to eggs just makes them rubbery, can lead to overcooking, and takes away from the delicious eggy flavor you want.

Cheesy Grits Breakfast Bowl

1 cup **whole milk**

2 tablespoons **unsalted butter**

1 tablespoon **sugar**

½ teaspoon **kosher salt**

½ cup **quick grits** (not instant)

1 cup **shredded cheddar cheese**

2 slices **thick-cut bacon**

2 **large eggs**

1 cup **cherry tomatoes**, sliced in half

1 **scallion**, white and green parts thinly sliced

Hot sauce, for serving

Helpful Hint

Slowly and steadily pouring while you whisk in the grits will ensure they are smooth, creamy, and free of lumps.

Grits were introduced to the American colonists by members of the Native American Muskogee tribe. The Muskogee homeland stretches from northern Florida, through Georgia and Alabama, up to southern Tennessee, so it's no surprise that 75 percent of America's grits consumption takes place in the South. Grits are a versatile blank canvas, perfect for breakfast, lunch, and dinner. Here we go into *full* breakfast mode for an extra-cheesy bowl of goodness topped with everything great.

1 In a medium saucepan, bring the milk, butter, sugar, salt, and 1 cup of water to a boil over medium-high heat. Whisking constantly, slowly pour in the grits and continue to whisk for about 1 minute. Reduce the heat to medium-low, cover, and cook for about 5 minutes, whisking halfway through, until the grits are tender. Remove the saucepan from the heat and add the cheese. Whisk 2 or 3 times to just barely distribute the cheese, but do not mix it in completely. Cover and set aside.

2 In a medium skillet, cook the bacon over medium heat for about 3 minutes, until golden brown on the bottom. Flip and cook for about 3 minutes more, until brown and crisp. Use tongs to transfer the bacon to a plate lined with paper towels.

3 Add the eggs and cherry tomatoes to the skillet. Fry the eggs for about 2 minutes, until the whites are just barely set. Remove from the heat.

4 Divide the grits into two bowls. Roughly chop the bacon and arrange over the top of the grits, along with the tomatoes and scallions. Rest an egg on top of each bowl and drizzle on some hot sauce before serving.

Iced Raspberry Danish

FOR THE DANISH

Nonstick cooking spray

1½ cups **all-purpose flour**

1 teaspoon **instant yeast**

½ teaspoon **kosher salt**

1 **large egg**

½ cup plus 1 tablespoon **whole milk**

¼ cup **granulated sugar**

4 tablespoons (½ stick) **unsalted butter,** at room temperature

1 cup **raspberry jam**

FOR THE CRUMBS

4 tablespoons (½ stick) **unsalted butter,** at room temperature

½ cup **all-purpose flour**

¼ cup **granulated sugar**

FOR THE ICING

1 cup **powdered sugar**

1 tablespoon **whole milk,** plus more as needed

Helpful Hint

A great place to proof dough is in the oven. It's a warm, draft-free spot that will guarantee a perfect rise every time. Just remember to pull the dough out before turning the oven on!

Funny story for word nerds: In Denmark, the term for Danish pastry is actually "Wienerbrød" (Viennese bread), named for the Austrian immigrants who introduced it to the region. But then Danish immigrants brought the pastry to the United States, so we call it a "Danish" on this side of the Atlantic. This easy homemade version of *that* raspberry Danish sold in the white box in grocery stores (you know the one) is a quick and easy way to total bliss. But be warned: There is no such thing as having just one slice!

1 Make the Danish: Spray a 9 by 13-inch baking pan with nonstick spray.

2 In a large bowl, whisk together the flour, yeast, and salt. Add the egg, ½ cup milk, and the granulated sugar and use a wooden spoon to stir until a sticky dough forms, about 3 minutes. Add the butter 1 tablespoon at a time and stir vigorously for 1 minute, until the butter is fully incorporated. Continue adding the butter and stirring until the dough is very soft and still a little sticky. (These steps can be done in a stand mixer on medium speed, if you have one.)

3 Spray a rubber spatula with nonstick spray and transfer the dough to the prepared baking pan. Smooth the dough into an even layer, stretching to make sure it covers the bottom of the pan. Cover with plastic wrap and let rise until puffy and bubbly, about 1 hour.

4 While the dough rises, make the crumbs: In a medium bowl, use clean hands to mash together the butter, flour, and granulated sugar to make a cohesive, crumbly mixture. Preheat the oven to 350°F and set a rack in the center.

5 Punch the dough down to deflate it completely. Spoon the raspberry jam in two long strips running the length of the baking pan. In a small bowl, stir together the remaining 1 tablespoon milk with 1 tablespoon of water, then brush the mixture over the dough. Cover with a damp towel and let rise for about 15 minutes, until the dough is starting to puff up again.

6 Bake for 25 to 30 minutes, until a toothpick inserted in the center comes out clean. Let cool completely in the pan, about 1 hour.

7 Make the icing: In a small bowl, whisk together the powdered sugar and tablespoon milk to form a thick icing. Add more milk, 1 teaspoon at a time, if needed. Transfer the icing to a small ziptop bag and snip off one corner to create a piping bag. Pipe the icing in large swoops across the Danish before serving.

New Jersey Crumb Buns

Serves 12

FOR THE CRUMB TOPPING

1 cup (2 sticks) **unsalted butter,** melted

1 packed cup **dark brown sugar**

½ cup **granulated sugar**

2 teaspoons **ground cinnamon**

½ teaspoon **kosher salt**

4 cups **all-purpose flour**

Powdered sugar, for serving

FOR THE BUNS

Nonstick cooking spray

2½ cups **all-purpose flour**

1 (¼-ounce) package **instant yeast**

1 teaspoon **kosher salt**

1 large **egg**

1 cup **whole milk**

¼ cup **granulated sugar**

6 tablespoons (¾ stick) **unsalted butter,** at room temperature

New Jersey crumb buns are a tradition all their own. Loaded with crumbs, but *not* in the shape of buns, they are like a coffee cake on steroids. A yeasty cake base gets piled high with a streusel topping (it seems like a lot, but just trust us on this one). Then—because why not?—the whole thing gets blanketed with powdered sugar. It's the definition of go big or go home!

1 Make the crumb topping: In a large bowl, whisk together the butter, brown sugar, granulated sugar, cinnamon, and salt. Sift in the flour and use a rubber spatula to fold the flour into the crumbly dough. Cover with plastic wrap and set aside.

2 Make the buns: Preheat the oven to 350°F and set a rack in the center. Spray a 9 by 13-inch baking pan with nonstick spray.

3 In a large bowl, whisk together the flour, yeast, and salt. Add the egg, milk, and granulated sugar and use a wooden spoon to stir until a sticky dough forms, about 3 minutes. Add the butter 1 tablespoon at a time and stir vigorously for 1 minute, until the butter is fully incorporated into the flour mixture. Continue adding the butter and stirring until the dough is very soft and still a little sticky. (These steps can be done in a stand mixer on medium speed, if you have one.)

4 Spray a rubber spatula with nonstick spray and use it to transfer the dough to the prepared baking pan. Smooth the dough into an even layer, stretching to make sure it covers the bottom of the pan. Cover with plastic wrap and let rise until puffy and slightly risen, about 1 hour.

5 Uncover the dough and the crumb topping. Squeeze handfuls of the crumb mixture together, then sprinkle over the dough in various-sized pieces. Transfer the pan to the oven and bake for 30 to 40 minutes, until a toothpick inserted in the center comes out clean. Cool completely in the pan, about 1 hour.

6 Slice the crumb buns into 12 equal pieces, then dust heavily with powdered sugar before serving.

Gravy-Stuffed Cheddar Biscuit Bombs

FOR THE GRAVY

8 ounces **breakfast sausage,** any casings removed

2 tablespoons **unsalted butter**

2 tablespoons **all-purpose flour**

1½ cups **whole milk**

½ teaspoon **kosher salt**

½ teaspoon **freshly ground black pepper**

½ teaspoon **ground sage**

½ teaspoon **dried thyme**

¼ teaspoon **red pepper flakes**

FOR THE BISCUITS

2 cups **all-purpose flour,** plus more as needed

1 tablespoon **baking powder**

½ cup (1 stick) **unsalted butter,** cut into cubes

1 cup **shredded cheddar cheese,** plus more as needed

2 tablespoons chopped **fresh chives**

1 teaspoon **kosher salt**

¾ cup **heavy cream**

1 large **egg,** lightly beaten

Chopped **fresh chives,** for serving

Helpful Hint

For the easiest way to cut out the biscuits, place some flour on a small plate and dip your biscuit cutter in the flour between each cut.

Biscuits and gravy, a classic of American cuisine, dates all the way back to the Revolutionary War, as it was an easy and filling breakfast that could be made from rations. The dish continued to grow in popularity, especially in southern Appalachian lumber camps, where it earned the nickname "sawmill gravy." And now it has reached its final form: biscuits *stuffed* with gravy. Imagine a cheesy, flaky biscuit that, in bite after bite, offers warm gravy goodness. A truly revolutionary breakfast!

1 Make the gravy: In a large skillet, cook the sausage over medium heat, breaking into small pieces, until evenly browned, about 5 minutes. Transfer to a medium bowl, leaving the fat in the skillet.

2 Add the butter to the skillet. When it has melted, add the flour and whisk until light golden brown, about 2 minutes. Slowly whisk in the milk, continously whisking until the gravy thickens, about 10 minutes. Stir in the salt, black pepper, sage, thyme, red pepper flakes, and sausage. Transfer the mixture to the bowl and let cool to room temperature.

3 Carefully spoon the cooled gravy into an ice cube tray to make 10 cubes and freeze overnight.

4 Make the biscuits: Preheat the oven to 350°F and set a rack in the center. Line a rimmed baking sheet with parchment paper.

5 Add the 2 cups flour, the baking powder, butter, 1 cup cheddar cheese, the chives, and salt to a food processor. Pulse about 8 times, until the mixture is coarse and crumbly. Add the cream and pulse until the dough comes together, about 6 more times. Turn the dough out onto a piece of plastic wrap and wrap tightly. Chill for 30 minutes in the refrigerator.

6 On a lightly floured surface, roll the dough out to about a ⅛-inch thickness and use a 4-inch biscuit cutter to cut 10 biscuits, rerolling the dough as needed. Remove the frozen gravy cubes from the ice cube tray and place 1 cube in the center of each biscuit circle. Bring the edges of the dough up over the gravy cube and roll to seal.

7 Place the stuffed biscuits on the prepared baking sheet. Brush with the beaten egg and sprinkle with more cheese. Bake the biscuits for 25 to 30 minutes, until golden brown. Cool for 10 minutes, then garnish with the chives and serve.

A

B

C

D

Lemon Poppy Seed Pancakes with Blueberry Syrup

FOR THE BLUEBERRY SYRUP

1 cup **pure maple syrup**

1 pint **fresh blueberries**

FOR THE PANCAKES

3 cups **all-purpose flour**

2 tablespoons **sugar**

2 tablespoons **poppy seeds**

2 teaspoons **baking powder**

1 teaspoon **baking soda**

½ teaspoon **kosher salt**

2 **large eggs**

2 cups **buttermilk**

4 tablespoons (½ stick) **unsalted butter**, melted

Grated **zest and juice of 2 lemons**

Nonstick cooking spray

Powdered sugar, for serving

Just thinking the words, "lemon poppy seed" can evoke longing for a sweetly iced pound cake or a warm muffin. There's no denying that lemon and poppy seeds are a signature flavor combination in American comfort food. And speaking of comfort, is anything better than whipping up a batch of pancakes on a weekend morning? (No, there is not.) This perfect stack is blanketed with a sweet and tangy blueberry syrup that only accents all the lemon-y goodness we already know and love. It is perfection on a plate.

1 Make the blueberry syrup: In a small saucepan, bring the maple syrup and half the blueberries to a simmer over medium heat. Stir occasionally, until the berries have burst open and the syrup is dark purple, about 10 minutes. Remove from the heat, add the remaining blueberries, and cover the pan.

2 Make the pancakes: Preheat the oven to 200°F and set a rack in the center. Place a rimmed baking sheet on the rack in the oven.

3 In a large bowl, whisk together the flour, sugar, poppy seeds, baking powder, baking soda, and salt. Add the eggs and beat just to break them up, then add the buttermilk, butter, and lemon zest and juice. Whisk to incorporate everything into a slightly lumpy batter.

4 Spray a large skillet with nonstick spray and set it over medium heat. When the skillet is warm, use a ½ cup measure to scoop the batter into the skillet. Cook until the top is bubbling, 2 to 3 minutes, then flip with a spatula and cook for 2 to 3 minutes more, until the bottom is golden brown. Transfer the finished pancake to the warm baking sheet in the oven while making the remaining pancakes.

5 When all the pancakes are done, divide them among six serving plates. Top each with the blueberry syrup and a dusting of the powdered sugar.

Sheet Pan Strawberry French Toast

Nonstick cooking spray

FOR THE TOPPING

2 cups sliced **fresh strawberries**

2 tablespoons **granulated sugar**

FOR THE TOAST

3 large **eggs**

1 tablespoon **vanilla extract**

1 tablespoon **light brown sugar**

1 teaspoon **ground cinnamon**

½ teaspoon **kosher salt**

2 tablespoons **unsalted butter**, melted

1 cup **whole milk**

8 slices **sandwich bread**

Room-temperature **unsalted butter, powdered sugar, and pure maple syrup, for serving**

The concept of bread soaked in milk and eggs, fried, and covered with something sweet dates all the way back to the Roman Empire. Fast-forward a few centuries, when the idea was perfected by the French and called pain perdu, a delicious solution for stale bread. And now we're taking things a step further by solving the eternal question: How do you feed a group while keeping all the servings warm? By baking this French toast all at once on a sheet tray! Everyone gets to eat together, and no one has to pop theirs into the microwave for a quick reheat. It's a solution even the Romans would love!

1 Preheat the oven to 400°F and set a rack in the lower third. Generously coat a rimmed baking sheet with nonstick spray (see Note).

2 Make the topping: In a medium bowl, toss the berries with the sugar. Set aside to macerate.

3 Make the toast: In a medium bowl, whisk together the eggs, vanilla, brown sugar, cinnamon, salt, and butter until the eggs are fully beaten. Add the milk and whisk to combine, then pour the egg mixture into the prepared baking sheet.

4 Lay each slice of bread in the egg mixture, then with a spatula immediately flip each piece in the same order as you laid them down. Let the bread slices absorb the egg mixture, about 30 seconds.

5 Bake the French toast for about 12 minutes, until the bottoms of the bread slices are golden brown. Carefully flip them over and bake for about 12 minutes more, until the other sides are golden brown as well.

6 Divide the French toast among the four serving plates. Add a pat of butter, top each with the macerated berries, and dust them with the powdered sugar. Serve with plenty of maple syrup.

Helpful Hint

Placing the oven rack in the lower third of the oven gives the toast more direct heat and better browning. Make sure to spray your baking sheet thoroughly so the bread slices flip easily!

Migas Breakfast Tacos

8 (8-inch) **flour tortillas**

2 tablespoons unsalted butter

8 large **eggs**

½ cup **chunky salsa** or **pico de gallo**

½ teaspoon **kosher salt**

½ teaspoon **freshly ground black pepper**

½ cup lightly crushed **corn tortilla chips**

¼ cup **shredded cheddar cheese**

Fresh cilantro leaves, avocado slices, and **hot sauce,** for serving

Helpful Hint

For a perfect scramble, stop cooking when the eggs are still a little runny. The heat in the pan will finish setting them, but the eggs will remain unbelievably soft and creamy.

Migas originated as a shepherd's dish in Spain and Portugal, a quick and hearty meal of stale bread plus heavily seasoned meat or vegetables. During the Spanish colonization of the Americas, migas were folded into Mexican cuisine as an egg dish with fried tortilla strips. Tex-Mex cuisine then upped the game by transforming migas into breakfast tacos with a wide variety of toppings. We like to keep it simple here, with a gooey scramble topped with a little salsa, a little cheese, and a lot of hot sauce. That translates to total comfort in any language.

1 Preheat the oven to 200°F and set a rack in the center.

2 Stack the tortillas and wrap them tightly in foil. Place the foil packet in the oven to warm.

3 In a large skillet, melt the butter over medium heat. In a large bowl, whisk together the eggs, salsa, salt, and pepper. Pour the egg mixture into the skillet and cook for about 1 minute, until the edges are beginning to set. Use a rubber spatula to gently push the eggs around in the skillet, forming large curds. When the eggs are almost set, about 2 minutes, sprinkle the tortilla chips and cheese over the eggs. Continue to stir gently for about 1 minute more, until the eggs are barely set and still soft (see Note). Remove from the heat.

4 Divide the tortillas among four serving plates. Evenly divide the eggs among the tortillas and top each with some cilantro, avocado, and hot sauce before serving.

Sugar & Spice Apple Cider Donuts

Nonstick cooking spray

1½ cups **apple cider**

4 tablespoons **dark brown sugar**

1 teaspoon **apple pie spice**
   (see Note)

1½ cups **all-purpose flour**

1 teaspoon **baking soda**

1 teaspoon **baking powder**

1 teaspoon **ground cinnamon**

½ teaspoon **kosher salt**

1 large **egg**

4 tablespoons (½ stick) **unsalted butter**, melted

¼ cup **granulated sugar**

Apple cider donuts are arguably the best part of fall (don't come for us PSL stans). A staple of farmers' markets and apple orchards in the Northeast, these light and cakey donuts are loaded with spices, blanketed with sugar, and best dunked in a mug of hot cider. Whip up a quick batch of these donuts and your house will be guaranteed fall vibes.

1 Preheat the oven to 350°F and set a rack in the center. Thoroughly coat two 6-cup donut pans with nonstick spray.

2 In a small saucepan, whisk together the apple cider, brown sugar, and apple pie spice. Bring to a boil over high heat, then reduce the heat to medium-low and simmer until the liquid is reduced to 1 cup, about 15 minutes. Pour the liquid into a measuring cup and let cool for 15 minutes.

3 In a large bowl, whisk together the flour, baking soda, baking powder, cinnamon, and salt. Add the cooled apple cider, the egg, and 2 tablespoons of the butter and stir to make a smooth batter. Spoon the batter evenly into the 12 donut cups (or bake in two batches, allowing the donut pan to cool before baking again).

4 Bake the donuts for 12 to 15 minutes, until they are golden brown and a toothpick inserted in the thickest part comes out clean. Let the donuts cool in the pan for 30 minutes.

5 Place the granulated sugar in a small bowl and pour the remaining 2 tablespoons melted butter in another small bowl. Remove a donut from the pan, brush with the melted butter, and dip in the granulated sugar to coat well. Place the donut on a serving plate and continue buttering and sugaring the remaining donuts. Serve while still warm.

Note: Make your own batch of apple pie spice by combining 3 tablespoons ground cinnamon in a small bowl with a teaspoon each ground nutmeg, ground allspice, ground ginger, and ground cardamom. Pour into an empty spice jar or airtight container for later use. Ground cinnamon alone will do the trick in a pinch.

Loco Moco

4 tablespoons (½ stick) **unsalted butter**

¼ cup finely diced **yellow onion**

½ cup roughly diced **cremini mushrooms**

Kosher salt and **freshly ground black pepper**

2 tablespoons **all-purpose flour**

2 cups **beef stock**

1 tablespoon **Worcestershire sauce**

1 (12-ounce) can **Spam**, cut into 8 slices

4 **large eggs**

2 cups **leftover cooked white rice**

Scallions, white and green parts thinly sliced, for serving

Loco moco is a contemporary Hawaiian plate of deliciousness, a perfect combo of white rice, brown gravy, a fried egg, and some kind of protein, often hamburger meat. (Is your stomach growling yet?) Variations can include bacon, teriyaki chicken, tofu, or seafood, but in a nod to Hawaii's favorite product, we're going with Spam. Loco moco can be enjoyed at any time of day, but here's a shout-out to all the savory breakfast lovers out there: This one is for you.

1 In a large skillet, melt 2 tablespoons of the butter over medium heat. Add the onion and cook, stirring occasionally, until softened, about 3 minutes. Add the mushrooms and continue to cook about 2 minutes more, until just starting to take some color. Season with salt and pepper.

2 Add the flour and stir to coat the mushrooms until no dry lumps of flour remain. Add the stock and Worcestershire sauce. Stir to combine well, then reduce the heat to low. Allow the gravy to simmer until thick and fragrant, about 10 minutes.

3 Meanwhile, in a medium skillet, melt 1 tablespoon of the butter over medium heat. Add the slices of Spam, working in batches if necessary, and fry for about 2 minutes on each side, until lightly browned and warmed through. Transfer to a plate.

4 In the same skillet, melt the remaining tablespoon butter. Add the eggs, season with salt and pepper, and cover. Cook for 2 to 3 minutes, until the whites are set but the yolks are still runny.

5 While the eggs cook, microwave the rice on high for about 2 minutes, until heated through. Divide the rice among four serving plates. Lay 2 pieces of spam over each mound of rice. Spoon the gravy over the Spam, then top each with a fried egg. Finish with a garnish of scallions and serve immediately.

Huevos Rancheros Breakfast Tostadas

1 (15.5-ounce) **can black beans**, drained and rinsed

½ teaspoon **kosher salt**, plus more as needed

½ teaspoon **dried oregano**

½ teaspoon **garlic powder**

½ teaspoon **onion powder**

½ teaspoon **ground cumin**

¼ teaspoon **cayenne pepper**

6 tablespoons **vegetable oil**

4 (6-inch) **corn tortillas**

4 large **eggs**

Diced **fresh tomato**, crumbled **cotija** or **feta cheese**, sliced **avocado**, **fresh cilantro leaves**, and **hot sauce**, for serving

The history of huevos rancheros is right in the translation of the name: eggs ranch style. A traditional Mexican breakfast on rural farms and ranches, huevos rancheros is commonly served over tortillas, smothered in salsa, and accompanied with beans, rice, and avocado. Tostadas, another example of Mexican perfection, are tortillas fried until crisp and topped with endless combinations of meat and vegetables. For a delicious start to the day, why not combine the best of both into one extraordinary breakfast?

1 Preheat the oven to 400°F and set a rack in the center. Line a rimmed baking sheet with parchment paper.

2 In a medium bowl, use a potato masher to mash the black beans into a chunky paste. Stir in the ½ teaspoon salt, the oregano, garlic powder, onion powder, cumin, and cayenne.

3 In a medium skillet, heat 2 tablespoons of the oil over medium heat. When the oil is shimmering, add 1 tortilla. Fry for about 2 minutes, until it is starting to brown on the bottom, then flip it over and fry for about 2 minutes more on the other side, until crisp. Transfer the fried tortilla to the prepared baking sheet. Fry another tortilla in the same oil and place on the baking sheet. Then add 2 more tablespoons of the oil and fry the remaining 2 tortillas, one at a time. Remove the skillet from the heat.

4 Spread the black bean mash evenly over the 4 tortillas on the baking sheet and bake for about 5 minutes, until the black beans are warmed through.

5 While the tortillas bake, crack all 4 eggs into a small bowl. Add the remaining 2 tablespoons oil to the skillet and return it to medium heat. When the oil is shimmering, gently pour the 4 eggs into the skillet and season with a pinch of salt. Fry for 3 to 4 minutes, until the whites are just set.

6 Remove the tostadas from the oven and divide onto two large plates. Place a fried egg on each tostada. Top each with some of the diced tomato, plenty of the cheese, the avocado, a sprinkle of the cilantro, and a drizzle of the hot sauce. Serve immediately.

Ginger Congee with Eggs & Scallion Oil

1 cup **long-grain white rice**

4 cups **chicken stock**

1 (2-inch) piece **fresh ginger**, peeled and grated

1 teaspoon **kosher salt**, or more as needed

4 **scallions**, white and green parts thinly sliced

¼ cup **raw sesame oil**

1 teaspoon **soy sauce**

4 **large eggs**

Helpful Hint

Why rinse the rice? Because otherwise the surface starch on the grains will make for gloopy and gummy rice. Without that excess starch the rice will cook evenly all the way through for a perfect pot every time.

Congee, a rice porridge dating all the way back to China's Zhou dynasty in 1000 BCE, is a staple of eastern and southern Asian and Asian American cuisine, with endless variations on preparations and seasoning. For those unfamiliar with it, congee offers the peak of total comfort, home cooking, love in a bowl—something soothing when you need it most. This recipe lightly infuses the rice with chicken stock and ginger, building a great base for plenty of savory toppings. We love a runny egg with a rich scallion oil, but let your stomach be your guide!

1 To a large bowl, add the rice and fill with cold water. Run your fingers through the rice to loosen the starch from the kernels. Drain and rinse, and repeat another two times to remove the starch. Drain thoroughly.

2 In a large pot, combine the stock, ginger, 1 teaspoon salt, and 2 cups of water. Bring the mixture to a boil over high heat, then add the rice. Reduce the heat to low, cover the pot halfway, and simmer for about 1 hour, stirring occasionally, until the rice is thick and creamy. Taste for salt and adjust as needed.

3 While the rice cooks, add the scallions to a small bowl. In a small saucepan, warm the sesame oil over medium-high heat. When the oil is shimmering, pour it over the scallions. Add the soy sauce and stir to combine.

4 Fill a medium saucepan with water and bring to a boil over high heat. Use a spoon to carefully lower the eggs into the water and boil for 7 minutes. Drain the eggs and immediately rinse under cold water to stop the cooking. When cool enough to handle, peel the eggs.

5 Divide the congee among four serving bowls. Slice the eggs in half and lay the halves on top of the congee. Drizzle the scallion oil over the top of each bowl and serve immediately.

Lunch Break

ULTIMATE AMERICAN SANDWICHES

each makes 2 sandwiches

All these sandwiches have two things in common. First, they have conflicting stories about their origins. Second, they are uniquely American creations. And they're all delicious—that's number three. The Cuban originated in Florida, either in Tampa, Miami, or on the Keys. The Reuben was born either in New York City or in Omaha, Nebraska. The two Melts have origin stories that can be traced all across the United States. But all four are staples of diners and delis everywhere in the country, making them deliciously and undoubtedly American.

Cuban

FOR THE PORK

- 1 pound **boneless pork tenderloin**, cut into 4 pieces
- **Kosher salt** and **freshly ground black pepper**
- Juice of 1 **lime**
- Juice of 1 navel **orange**
- 1 **garlic clove**, grated
- ¼ teaspoon **dried oregano**
- ¼ teaspoon **ground cumin**
- 1 tablespoon **vegetable oil**

FOR THE SANDWICH

- 1 loaf **Cuban** or **Italian bread**
- 4 tablespoons **yellow mustard**
- 8 ounces sliced **Swiss cheese**
- 8 ounces sliced **smoked ham**
- 4 **sandwich pickles**
- 1 tablespoon **unsalted butter**

1. Make the pork: Pat dry the pork and season all over with salt and pepper. In a small bowl, whisk together the lime juice, orange juice, garlic, oregano, and cumin.

2. In a medium skillet, heat the oil over medium-high heat. Add the pork and sear for about 5 minutes on one side, until nicely browned, then flip over and sear for 5 minutes more on the other side. Reduce the heat to medium-low and add the seasoning mix. Cover and simmer for about 15 minutes, until the pork is cooked through. Transfer to a plate and pour the seasoned juices over the top.

3. Cut the loaf in half vertically, then slice each piece in half horizontally to make 4 sandwich halves. Spread the mustard on all 4 halves, then layer the cheese and ham on the bottom halves. Lay the sandwich pickles on the top halves.

4. Thinly slice the pork and divide between the 2 sandwiches. Drizzle some of the juices over the pork, then close the sandwiches and press down on the tops.

5. Melt the butter over medium heat in the same skillet as used for the pork. Add the 2 sandwiches, then place a smaller cast-iron skillet or heavy pot on top of them to press them down. Fry for about 4 minutes, until the bread is lightly browned and the cheese has started to melt. Flip the sandwiches over and return the smaller skillet to the sandwich tops to press down again. Fry for about 4 minutes more, until the cheese is fully melted and the sandwiches are nice and flat. Serve immediately.

Reuben

- 4 tablespoons (½ stick) **unsalted butter**, at room temperature
- 4 slices **rye bread**
- 2 tablespoons **Thousand Island dressing**
- 8 slices **Swiss cheese**
- 8 ounces **sliced corned beef**
- ½ cup **sauerkraut**

1. Set a large skillet over medium heat.

2. Butter both sides of the bread slices, and lay them out on a work surface. Spread the dressing on top of each piece of bread. Lay the cheese slices on top of the bread slices. Layer the corned beef and sauerkraut onto 2 of the slices, then press the remaining slices on top, creating 2 sandwiches.

3. Transfer the sandwiches to the warm skillet. Fry for about 4 minutes, until the bottom slices are crisp and golden brown. Flip over and fry on the other side for about 4 minutes more, until the cheese is melted and the bottom slices are golden brown. Serve immediately.

Patty Melt

8 ounces **ground beef**

1 teaspoon **onion powder**

1 teaspoon **garlic powder**

½ teaspoon **kosher salt**

¼ teaspoon **freshly ground black pepper**

1 tablespoon **Worcestershire sauce**

1 tablespoon **unsalted butter**

4 tablespoons **mayonnaise**

4 slices hearty **sandwich bread,** such as rye or whole wheat

4 slices **cheddar cheese**

Caramelized onions (optional; see page 101)

1 In a medium bowl, use clean hands to mix the ground beef, onion powder, garlic powder, salt, pepper, and Worcestershire sauce. Roll the beef into 2 equal-sized balls.

2 In a large skillet, melt the butter over medium-high heat. Press the balls into patties, then place the patties in the hot skillet. Sear for about 2 minutes, until the bottoms are nicely browned. Then flip over with a spatula and sear for about 2 minutes more on the other side for medium-rare or 4 minutes for well done.

3 Meanwhile, spread the mayonnaise on both sides of the bread slices. Place a slice of the cheese on each bread slice, then divide the caramelized onions (if using) among the slices. Place the seared burgers on 2 of the bread pieces, then press the remaining bread pieces on top, creating 2 sandwiches.

4 Lower the heat under the skillet to medium and transfer the sandwiches to the warm pan. Fry the sandwiches for about 3 minutes, until the bottom slices are crisp and golden brown. Flip over with a spatula and fry on the other side for about 3 minutes more, until the cheese is melted and the bottom slices are golden brown. Serve immediately.

Tuna Melt

¼ cup **mayonnaise**

1 (6-ounce) can **tuna**, drained

1 **celery stalk**, finely chopped

1 **dill pickle**, finely chopped

1 tablespoon chopped **fresh parsley**

¼ teaspoon **kosher salt**

¼ teaspoon **freshly ground black pepper**

4 tablespoons (½ stick) **unsalted butter,** at room temperature

4 slices hearty **sandwich bread,** such as rye or whole wheat

4 slices **cheddar cheese**

1 small **ripe tomato**, thinly sliced

1 In a medium bowl, mix the mayonnaise, tuna, celery, pickle, parsley, salt, and pepper.

2 Set a large skillet over medium heat. Butter both sides of each slice of bread and lay the slices out on a work surface. Lay a cheese slice and a tomato slice on top of each bread slice. Scoop the tuna mixture onto 2 of the slices, then press the other slices down onto the tuna, creating 2 complete sandwiches.

3 Transfer the sandwiches to the warm skillet. Fry for about 4 minutes, until the bottom of each is crisp and golden brown. Flip over with a spatula and fry for about 4 minutes more, until the cheese is melted and the bottom slice is golden brown. Serve immediately.

Matzo Ball Soup

FOR THE MATZO BALLS

3 large eggs

¼ cup **vegetable oil** or **schmaltz**

1 teaspoon **kosher salt**

½ teaspoon **freshly ground black pepper**

½ teaspoon **baking powder**

¾ cup **matzo meal**

3 tablespoons **seltzer**

FOR THE SOUP

1 tablespoon **vegetable oil** or **schmaltz**

1 small **yellow onion**, finely chopped

2 quarts **chicken broth**

1 pound **skin-on chicken thighs**

Kosher salt and **freshly ground black pepper**

2 medium **carrots**, finely chopped

2 **celery stalks**, finely chopped

1 medium **parsnip**, peeled and finely chopped

Fresh dill sprigs, for serving

Helpful Hint

For those out of the loop, schmaltz is rendered chicken fat and a traditional ingredient in Ashkenazi Jewish cooking. Super flavorful, rich, and versatile, schmaltz can be everything from a key ingredient to the shimmering pool of fat you use to fry.

The origins of matzo ball soup are difficult to trace. The industrialization of matzo production during the 1800s created an abundance of matzo crumbs and meal, leading to their use in making matzo balls—an ingenious solution that became a staple of Jewish culture. From there, the light and fluffy balls found their way into steaming bowls of chicken soup, and history was made. When we're talking about total comfort, matzo ball soup is it. It's pure family, pure love, pure bubbe vibes, and this is a soup everyone will love, Jewish or not.

1 Make the matzo balls: In a medium bowl, whisk together the eggs, oil, salt, pepper, and baking powder. Add the matzo meal and stir until blended. Add the seltzer and stir to form a smooth mixture. Cover and refrigerate for 30 minutes to allow the matzo meal to thicken.

2 Meanwhile, make the soup: Heat the oil in a Dutch oven or large pot over medium-high heat. When the oil is shimmering, add the onion and cook, stirring occasionally, for about 5 minutes, until the onion starts to soften. Add the broth and bring to a boil.

3 Season both sides of the chicken thighs with salt, then add to the broth. Cover and reduce the heat to low. Simmer for about 8 minutes, until the chicken is cooked through. Using tongs, remove the chicken to a cutting board. Skim off any foam that has formed on the top of the broth.

4 Remove the matzo ball dough from the refrigerator. Scoop up about 2 tablespoons and roll it into a Ping-pong–sized ball. Set on a plate and continue rolling the matzo balls.

5 Increase the heat to high under the Dutch oven and return the broth to a boil. Add the carrots, celery, and parsnip and season well with salt and pepper. Drop in the matzo balls, then cover the pot and reduce the heat to low. Simmer the soup for 25 to 30 minutes, until the matzo balls are light and fluffy.

6 While the matzo balls cook, remove the skin from the chicken pieces and shred the meat. When the soup is ready, add the chicken and simmer on low heat for 2 minutes to heat through. Divide the soup and matzo balls among serving bowls and serve with fresh dill.

Cafeteria Pizza

Serves 8

FOR THE DOUGH

1 tablespoon **sugar**

1 (¼-ounce) packet **active dry yeast**

¼ cup **olive oil,** plus more as needed

2 teaspoons **kosher salt**

4 cups **all-purpose flour**

Nonstick cooking spray

FOR THE SAUCE

1 (28-ounce) can **whole peeled tomatoes,** drained

1 teaspoon **kosher salt**

2 whole **garlic cloves**

½ teaspoon **fennel seeds**

½ teaspoon **dried basil**

½ teaspoon **dried oregano**

½ teaspoon **onion powder**

FOR THE PIZZA

2 cups **shredded mozzarella cheese**

Olive oil and **flaky sea salt,** for serving

Many of us grew up with Pizza Day at school, when we were served long, doughy rectangles of bread, sauce, cheese, and maybe a pepperoni or two. But that style of pizza stretches back to Sicily of the 1800s, when the formula was basically a focaccia with toppings. Sicilian immigrants brought the tradition to America, where this doughy style of pizza was often known as "grandma pizza," a nod to the older generation's preservation of a food they loved, adapted to American ovens and ingredients. So, following the wisdom of school lunch ladies and Sicilian nonnas everywhere, bake a mega-sized pizza to have a smart, easy, and delicious way to feed a crowd!

1 Make the dough: In a large bowl, whisk the sugar with 2 cups of warm water until dissolved. Sprinkle the packet of yeast on top and let sit for 5 minutes while the yeast blooms.

2 Add the ¼ cup olive oil, the salt, and flour to the yeast mixture and stir to create a cohesive dough. Coat one hand with some olive oil and knead the dough in the bowl about 2 minutes, to create a sticky, stretchy dough. Cover the bowl with plastic wrap and chill in the refrigerator for 8 hours, or up to 24 hours.

3 Thoroughly coat a rimmed baking sheet with nonstick spray. Scrape the dough out of the bowl and onto the baking sheet, then let it rest for 20 minutes to come to room temperature. Gently press the dough to stretch it across the baking sheet. Stop to let it rest more if you find it is springing back at your touch. Cover the dough with plastic wrap and let rise in a warm place until puffy and bubbly, about 30 minutes.

4 Preheat the oven to 500°F and set a rack in the lower third of the oven.

5 Make the sauce: In a blender or food processor, combine the tomatoes, salt, garlic, fennel, basil, oregano, and onion powder. Blend on high speed to form a smooth sauce, about 2 minutes.

6 When the dough has risen, make the pizza: Spoon the sauce over the dough, being careful not to deflate the dough. Transfer the pizza to the oven and bake for 15 minutes. Remove it from the oven and sprinkle the cheese over the sauce. Place it back in the oven and bake for 10 to 12 minutes more, until the crust is crisp on the bottom and the cheese is bubbling on top. Drizzle with a little olive oil and sprinkle with sea salt before slicing and serving.

Korean Hot Dogs

Makes 8 hot dogs

FOR THE BATTER

2 tablespoons **sugar**

1 (¼-ounce) packet **active dry yeast**

2 teaspoons **kosher salt**

3½ cups **all-purpose flour**

FOR THE HOT DOGS

4 **hot dogs**

4 strips of **string cheese**

2 pounds **russet potatoes**, cut into ¼-inch cubes

1½ cups **panko crumbs**

2 quarts **vegetable oil**

Sugar, ketchup, and **yellow mustard**, for serving

Sometimes America reinterprets foreign foods, and sometimes other countries reinterpret American favorites. Case in point: the South Korean snack known as "gamja-hotdog." Somewhere between a corn dog on a stick and a hot dog with a side of fries, this dish is truly an all-in-one package deal. The hot dog gets skewered along with some cheese, then is rolled in dough, loaded with potato pieces, deep fried, and finally is sprinkled with sugar and drizzled with ketchup and mustard. In a full-circle moment, gamja-hotdogs have become the next big culinary trend in America, now sold as "Korean corn dogs" across the country. After one bite, it will be obvious why this crunchy, savory, sweet, and very satisfying dog is such a hit around the globe.

1 Make the batter: In a large bowl, whisk the sugar with 2 cups of warm water until dissolved. Sprinkle the packet of yeast on top and let sit for 5 minutes for the yeast to bloom.

2 Add the salt and flour to the yeast mixture and stir to create a sticky dough. Cover and let rest somewhere warm until doubled in size, about 1 hour.

3 Make the hot dogs: Lay the hot dogs and cheese strips on a cutting board. Slice each into 4 equal pieces, then rearrange the pieces to create 8 rows of alternating hot dog and cheese pieces. Skewer the contents of each row onto a chopstick.

4 Spread the potato cubes on a large plate. On another large plate, spread the panko.

5 Heat the oil in a Dutch oven or large heavy saucepan over medium-high heat. Use an instant-read thermometer to check periodically until the oil hits 350°F.

6 Working in pairs, dip 2 skewers in the risen dough, swirling to coat each skewer completely. Roll each battered skewer in the potatoes, pressing to make sure the potato pieces stick to the batter. Then roll the skewers in the panko to completely coat with the crumbs. Using tongs, place the skewers in the hot oil and fry for about 5 minutes, turning them over halfway through, until golden brown on all sides. Set aside to drain on paper towels while you batter and coat the remaining skewers, then fry them in the hot oil until crisp.

7 Sprinkle the warm hot dogs with plenty of sugar, then give them a good drizzle of ketchup and mustard before serving.

Chicken Fried Steak & Gravy

FOR THE STEAKS

2 large **eggs**

1 cup **whole milk**

1½ cups **all-purpose flour**

1 teaspoon **garlic powder**

1 teaspoon **onion powder**

1 teaspoon **smoked paprika**

1 teaspoon **kosher salt**, plus more as needed

½ teaspoon **freshly ground black pepper**, plus more as needed

4 (8-ounce) **cube steaks**

1 cup **vegetable oil**

FOR THE GRAVY

3 tablespoons **unsalted butter**

3 tablespoons **all-purpose flour**

1 cup **whole milk**

½ cup **heavy cream**

½ teaspoon **kosher salt**

½ teaspoon **freshly ground black pepper**

Chopped **fresh parsley**, for serving

The origin of chicken fried steak can possibly be traced to German and Austrian immigrants in Texas, who brought their love of schnitzel, a pounded, breaded, and fried pork or veal cutlet, to their new home. Here, a thin beef steak gets dredged in a seasoned coating, fried like chicken pieces, and then blanketed with a creamy, rich gravy. It's a decadent, hardy dish that is a staple of home cooking and offers the peak of comfort.

1 Make the steaks: Preheat the oven to 200°F and set a rack in the center. Set a wire rack into a rimmed baking sheet, then place the baking sheet in the oven to warm.

2 In a wide, shallow dish, whisk together the eggs and milk. In another shallow dish, stir together the flour, garlic powder, onion powder, paprika, the 1 teaspoon salt, and the ½ teaspoon pepper.

3 Set 1 steak in the center of a cutting board and cover it with a piece of plastic wrap. Using a meat mallet or rolling pin, pound the steak evenly to a ¼-inch thickness. Set on a plate and repeat with the remaining steaks.

4 Pat the flattened steaks dry on both sides with paper towels and season generously with salt and pepper. Dredge the steaks in the flour mixture, then dip in the egg mixture, letting any excess egg drip off. Coat again in the flour mixture. Set aside for 10 to 15 minutes so the coating has time to dry a bit.

5 Meanwhile, heat the oil in a 10-inch skillet over medium-high heat. Use an instant-read thermometer and periodically check until the oil hits 375°F. Fry the steaks 2 at a time until golden brown and crispy, about 3 minutes per side. Transfer to the prepared baking sheet in the oven to keep warm while frying the remaining 2 steaks.

6 Make the gravy: Pour off the oil in the skillet, but leave any browned bits. Add the butter and melt it over medium heat. Add the flour, whisking to incorporate, and cook for 2 to 3 minutes, until the roux is golden brown and smells toasty. Add the milk, cream, salt, and pepper. Bring to a simmer and cook, whisking constantly, until gravy is thickened, 5 to 7 minutes.

7 Arrange the steaks on four serving plates and ladle the gravy over them. Garnish with fresh parsley and serve immediately.

Spicy Tortellini & Sausage Soup

1 tablespoon **olive oil**

1 pound **spicy Italian sausage,** casings removed

1 medium **yellow onion,** finely chopped

4 **garlic cloves,** thinly sliced

2 tablespoons **tomato paste**

4 cups **chicken stock**

1 (14.5-ounce) can **diced tomatoes**

2 teaspoons **kosher salt,** or more as needed

1 teaspoon **freshly ground black pepper,** or more as needed

6 cups stemmed and roughly chopped **fresh kale**

1 (9-ounce) package **tortellini**

1 cup **heavy cream**

Grated **Parmesan cheese** and chopped **fresh basil leaves,** for serving

Tortellini, originating in Italy's Emilia-Romagna region, are traditionally stuffed with meat and served in a light chicken broth. But what is tradition if not the foundation for invention? This recipe flips the script, taking the traditional preparation to the bowl-filling max with a creamy soup loaded with sausage, tomatoes, kale, and (we didn't forget!) tortellini. When everyone at the table is asking for seconds, you know it's got to be good.

1 Heat the olive oil in a Dutch oven or large heavy pot over medium-high heat. When the oil is shimmering, add the sausage and onion. Cook, stirring and breaking up with a wooden spoon, until the sausage is starting to brown, but not yet cooked through, 2 to 3 minutes. Add the garlic and cook 1 minute more, until fragrant.

2 Add the tomato paste and cook, stirring occasionally, until the paste is a deep red, about 5 minutes. Add the stock, tomatoes, 2 teaspoons salt, and 1 teaspoon pepper. Bring to a rapid simmer and cook for about 15 minutes, until the flavors have melded. Add the kale and tortellini, and simmer for about 5 minutes, until the tortellini are tender.

3 Remove the pot from the heat and stir in the cream. Taste for seasoning, then divide into serving bowls. Serve with the grated Parmesan and chopped basil.

Fried Chicken Adobo

FOR THE MARINADE

10 garlic cloves, smashed

6 dried bay leaves or **3 fresh bay leaves**

1 heaping tablespoon whole black peppercorns

1 teaspoon kosher salt

½ cup unseasoned **rice vinegar** or **coconut vinegar**

½ cup soy sauce

½ cup full-fat coconut milk

2 pounds chicken thighs and **drumsticks**

FOR THE FRIED CHICKEN

2 cups all-purpose flour

1 tablespoon kosher salt

1 tablespoon freshly ground black pepper

1 tablespoon garlic powder

2 quarts vegetable oil

Scallions, green parts only thinly sliced, for serving

Helpful Hint

When coating the chicken for frying, use one hand to handle the wet (marinade) and one hand for the dry (flour). It'll keep your fingers from getting coated and gummy.

Chicken adobo, a perfect stew of tender chicken, tangy vinegar, savory soy sauce, plus flavor boosts from garlic, peppercorns, and bay leaves, is unofficially the national dish of the Philippines. A classic cooking method for generations of indigenous Filipinos, it is still one of the great culinary prides of Filipino home cooking. This fried chicken recipe merges all the fantastic flavors of a traditional adobo with a satisfyingly crunchy chicken, plus a bonus drizzle of adobo sauce over the top because, let's be honest, the sauce is the best part.

1 Make the marinade: In a large ziptop bag, combine the garlic, bay leaves, peppercorns, salt, vinegar, soy sauce, coconut milk, and chicken. Seal the bag and shake to thoroughly coat the chicken with the marinade. Lay the bag flat on a shelf in the refrigerator and chill for at least 1 hour or up to 24 hours.

2 Make the fried chicken: Preheat the oven to 200°F and set a rack in the center of the oven. Set a wire rack on top of a rimmed baking sheet.

3 In a large bowl, whisk together the flour, salt, pepper, and garlic powder.

4 Remove the chicken from the marinade and set on a plate. Strain the marinade into a medium saucepan, discarding the garlic, bay leaves, and peppercorns.

5 Heat the oil in a Dutch oven or large heavy saucepan over medium-high heat. Use an instant-read thermometer to check periodically until the oil reaches 350°F.

6 Working in batches, dip the chicken pieces into the marinade, then toss in the flour mixture to coat (see Note). Dip the coated chicken back into the marinade and once more toss the chicken in the flour. Transfer about one-fourth of the chicken pieces to the hot oil and fry for 5 to 7 minutes, until the chicken is dark golden brown and cooked through. Transfer the fried chicken to the prepared baking sheet and keep warm in the oven while you fry the remaining chicken pieces, in batches.

7 When finished frying, set the remaining marinade over medium-high heat. Simmer, stirring occasionally, until reduced by half and it is a thick, dark sauce, about 5 minutes.

8 Transfer the chicken to a serving plate. Drizzle the sauce over the top and finish with a sprinkle of scallion greens. Serve immediately.

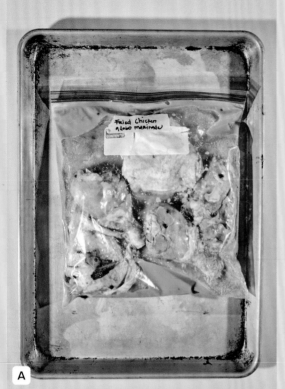

Haitian Macaroni au Gratin

Serves 6 to 8

Nonstick cooking spray

1 pound **rigatoni**

2 tablespoons **unsalted butter**

½ cup finely chopped **green bell pepper**

½ cup finely chopped **red bell pepper**

½ cup finely chopped **yellow onion**

2 **garlic cloves**, finely chopped

Kosher salt and **freshly ground black pepper**

1 (12-ounce) can **evaporated milk** (see Note)

8 ounces **cheddar cheese**, grated

4 ounces **smoked Gouda cheese**, grated

4 ounces **Parmesan cheese**, grated

Helpful Hint

Make sure to buy evaporated milk, a canned milk product with less water, and not sweetened condensed milk, which has sugar added. The cans usually are right next to each other, in similar packaging, so it's worth double checking.

The exact evolution of Haitian-style macaroni au gratin is hard to trace, but after 150 years of French colonial rule, it's safe to guess how the creamy sauce and the "au gratin" topping came into play. There are as many variations of macaroni au gratin as there are Haitian home cooks. Some families add ham, some add mayo, and despite the name, many people use rigatoni in place of macaroni, as done here. But no matter how you make it, this is a creamy, delicious dish offering total comfort.

1 Preheat the oven to 350°F and set a rack in the center. Spray a 9 by 13-inch baking pan with nonstick spray.

2 Bring a large pot of salted water to a boil over high heat, then add the rigatoni. Cook about 2 minutes past what would be al dente according the package instructions, until the noodles are a little soft. Drain.

3 In a Dutch oven or large heavy pot, melt the butter over medium heat. Add the green and red peppers, the onion, and garlic, along with a generous pinch of salt and pepper. Cook, stirring occasionally, until the peppers and onion are soft, about 8 minutes.

4 Reduce the heat to low. Add the pasta and about ¼ cup of the evaporated milk. Stir well for about 1 minute to release the starch in the pasta, thickening the liquid. Add about half the cheeses and about 1 cup more of the evaporated milk. Continue stirring to melt the cheeses and agitate the pasta starch, about 2 minutes more, to create a smooth and very thick sauce. Add the remaining ¼ cup evaporated milk and stir to combine.

5 Pour the mixture into the prepared baking pan. Sprinkle the remaining cheeses over the top. Bake for 35 to 40 minutes, until the top is golden brown and bubbly. Serve immediately.

Fish Sticks & Tangy Tartar Sauce

FOR THE SAUCE

1 cup **mayonnaise**

½ small **shallot**, minced

¼ cup minced **dill pickle**

2 tablespoons drained **capers**, minced

2 tablespoons finely chopped **fresh parsley**

1 tablespoon **Dijon mustard**

1 teaspoon **freshly ground black pepper**

½ teaspoon **kosher salt**

FOR THE FISH

1 cup **all-purpose flour**

½ teaspoon **onion powder**

½ teaspoon **garlic powder**

2 teaspoons **kosher salt**

2 **large eggs**

2 cups **panko crumbs**

½ teaspoon **smoked paprika**

½ teaspoon **ground cumin**

½ teaspoon **dried oregano**

¼ teaspoon **cayenne pepper**

1 pound **cod fillets**

2 cups **vegetable oil**

England gave us fish and chips, but the American food industry in the 1950s gave us the boxes of frozen fish sticks we loved as kids. This recipe lands somewhere between the joys of childhood and the satisfaction of adulthood, with easy fried fish sticks and a tangy tartar sauce that begs for double dipping. They're better than those in the box, oh-fish-ally!

1 Make the sauce: In a small bowl, whisk together the mayonnaise, shallot, pickle, capers, parsley, mustard, pepper, and salt. Cover with plastic wrap and refrigerate.

2 Make the fish: In a shallow bowl, whisk together the flour, onion powder, garlic powder, and ½ teaspoon of the salt. In a second shallow bowl, thoroughly whisk the eggs and ½ teaspoon of the salt. In a third shallow bowl, stir together the panko, paprika, cumin, oregano, cayenne, and ½ teaspoon of the salt.

3 Pat the fish dry and season both sides with the remaining ½ teaspoon salt. Slice the fillets crosswise into 1-inch-wide strips. Dredge each piece of fish in the flour, shaking off the excess. Then coat in the egg, allowing the excess to drip off. Then roll in the panko, patting to adhere the crumbs.

4 In a large deep skillet, heat the vegetable oil over medium-high heat. Do the chopstick test (see Helpful Hint) or sprinkle a few panko crumbs on the surface of the oil to check the temperature. Use tongs to lower half the fish sticks into the hot oil. Fry for 2 to 3 minutes on each side, turning over with the tongs, until golden brown. Transfer the fish to a plate lined with paper towels, and fry the remaining fish sticks.

5 Arrange the fish sticks on a serving platter with the bowl of chilled sauce alongside. Serve immediately.

Helpful Hint

Dip the tip of a chopstick (or sprinkle some panko) in the oil in the skillet. If the bubbles that form are rapid and steady, but not too aggressive, the oil is ready for frying. Of course, an instant-read thermometer is always an option—we're aiming for 350°F.

Wedge Salad with Creamy Blue Cheese Dressing

FOR THE DRESSING

1 cup **mayonnaise**

½ cup **sour cream**

¼ cup **buttermilk**

2 tablespoons **fresh lemon juice**

2 teaspoons **garlic powder**

1 teaspoon **onion powder**

1 teaspoon **freshly ground black pepper**

½ teaspoon **celery salt**

¼ teaspoon **cayenne pepper**

1 cup **crumbled blue cheese**

FOR THE SALAD

2 cups (1 pint) **cherry tomatoes,** sliced in half

1 **shallot,** thinly sliced

2 tablespoons **fresh lemon juice**

1 tablespoon **olive oil**

Kosher salt and **freshly ground black pepper**

4 slices **thick-cut bacon,** cut into ½-inch pieces

1 large head **iceberg lettuce,** cut into 4 wedges

The history of salad starts with the ancient Egyptians, who we can thank for cultivating the first lettuce crops. Lettuce plants evolved through many centuries and during lots of fallen empires, until they landed on American shores along with the European colonists. But it wasn't until the 1920s that an ingenious invention, the wedge salad, started to show up in restaurants. Bacon and blue cheese dressing joined the party in the 1950s, and the 1970s cemented its status as *the* steakhouse starter. Now in the 2020s, we're reclaiming the wedge salad as a perfect (and perfectly delicious) lunch, at home or packed to go. We've come a long way!

1   Make the dressing: In a medium bowl, whisk together the mayonnaise, sour cream, buttermilk, lemon juice, garlic powder, onion powder, pepper, celery salt, and cayenne. Gently fold in the blue cheese.

2   Make the salad: In a medium bowl, combine the cherry tomatoes and shallot. Toss with the lemon juice, olive oil, and a heavy pinch of salt and pepper. Let marinate for 10 minutes.

3   Arrange the bacon pieces in an even layer in a large skillet. Set the skillet over medium heat and cook, stirring occasionally, until the bacon is crisp, about 8 minutes. Transfer the bacon to a plate lined with paper towels to drain.

4   Lay each wedge of lettuce sideways on each of four serving plates. Top with some of the tomatoes and shallot, then sprinkle on some bacon. Spoon the dressing over each serving and finish with a generous grinding of black pepper. Serve immediately.

New England Clam Chowdah

4 slices **thick-cut bacon**, chopped

2 **celery stalks**, chopped

1 large **white onion**, chopped

1 **garlic clove**, minced

½ teaspoon **freshly ground black pepper**, plus more as needed

½ teaspoon **dried thyme**

1 tablespoon **kosher salt**

1 pound **russet potatoes**, cut into ½-inch cubes

2 (8-ounce) bottles **clam juice**

2 cups **chicken stock**

2 tablespoons **all-purpose flour**

¼ cup (½ stick) **unsalted butter**, at room temperature

2 cups **half-and-half**

2 (6.5-ounce) cans **chopped clams**, drained

Chopped **fresh chives** and **oyster crackers**, for serving

Clam chowder was likely a creation of the Portuguese fishing communities along coastal New England, and early versions of the soup were thickened with crushed crackers or stale bread. (See the history of soup on page 100.) These days, there are many styles of clam chowder served along the coastal northeastern United States. There's Manhattan style (tomato broth), Long Island style (tomato and cream broth), and Rhode Island style (clear broth). But the warmest and most comforting version is the traditional New England–style clam chowder. Creamy and rich, with just enough briny ocean flavor, this is the perfect bowl of comfort on a chilly day.

1 Add the bacon to a Dutch oven or large heavy pot. Set over medium heat and stir while the bacon renders its fat. Continue to cook, stirring occasionally, until the bacon is crisp, about 5 minutes. Add the celery, onion, and garlic. Continue to cook, stirring occasionally, until the onion is translucent, about 10 minutes.

2 Stir in the ½ teaspoon pepper and the thyme, heating for about 30 seconds, until fragrant. Add the salt, potatoes, clam juice, and stock and stir to combine. Bring the soup to a simmer, then cover and cook until the potatoes are tender, about 20 minutes.

3 In a small bowl, use a fork to mash the flour and butter together, until the flour is fully incorporated into the butter (see Note). Add the mixture to the soup and simmer until soup is thickened, about 2 minutes more. Remove from the heat and stir in the half-and-half and clams.

4 Divide the soup among four bowls. Serve with a sprinkle of chives, a good grinding of black pepper, and the oyster crackers.

Helpful Hint

A mixture of flour and butter, a French technique called beurre manié, is an easy way to thicken a soup or stew without introducing clumps of flour. Make sure the flour is completely incorporated into the butter for a smooth, shiny finish to the soup.

Vegan Bánh Mì

FOR THE TOFU

¼ cup **tamari** or **soy sauce**

1 tablespoon **dark brown sugar**

1 **garlic clove**, grated

1 (1-inch) piece **fresh ginger**, peeled and grated

Zest and juice of 1 **lime**

8 ounces (½ block) **extra-firm tofu**, cut into 4 slices

FOR THE PICKLE

½ cup **unseasoned rice vinegar**

1 teaspoon **kosher salt**

1 tablespoon **granulated sugar**

¼ cup **julienned carrot**

¼ cup thinly sliced **radishes**

½ cup **boiling water**

FOR THE SPICY MAYO

½ cup **vegan mayonnaise**

1 tablespoon **sriracha** (see Note)

FOR THE CAULIFLOWER

1 tablespoon **vegetable oil**

½ medium head **fresh cauliflower**, cored and cut into florets

2 tablespoons **chili garlic sauce**

¼ cup **tamari** or **soy sauce**

Juice of 1 **lime**

The Vietnamese words bánh mì simply translate to "bread." But the meaning *behind* the meaning is a short, crunchy baguette transformed into a sandwich with incredible amounts of flavors and textures. Fillings can range from meatballs to sardines, to fried eggs, to ice cream. But traditional Vietnamese cooking follows a philosophy of including five tastes—spicy, sour, bitter, salty, and sweet—that perfectly balance a dish. This vegan take on bánh mì layers those five flavors and a variety of textures for a sandwich that's total comfort to the last bite.

1 Make the tofu: In a small bowl, whisk together the tamari, brown sugar, garlic, ginger, and lime. Arrange the tofu slices in an even layer on a large plate and pour the sauce over, turning the slices in the sauce. Let marinate at room temperature for 20 minutes, flipping the tofu again halfway through.

2 Make the pickle: In a medium jar or bowl, combine the vinegar, salt, granulated sugar, carrot, and radishes. Pour in the boiling water and stir to dissolve the sugar and salt. Cover with a lid or plastic wrap.

3 Make the spicy mayo: In a small bowl, whisk together the mayonnaise and sriracha.

4 Make the cauliflower: In a large nonstick skillet, heat the oil over medium-high heat. When the oil is shimmering, add the cauliflower florets in an even layer. Cook undisturbed for about 5 minutes, until florets are charred on one side.

5 Meanwhile, in a medium bowl, whisk together the chili garlic sauce, tamari, and lime juice. Pour the mixture over the charred cauliflower in the skillet and scrape up any browned bits from the pan. Continue to cook, stirring occasionally, until the cauliflower is tender and the sauce has thickened, about 2 minutes. Transfer the cauliflower to the bowl used to mix the sauce.

1 tablespoon unsalted butter, at room temperature

2 demi baguettes, cut in half

2 tablespoons vegetable oil

Fresh cilantro leaves, julienned **cucumber,** and thinly sliced **jalapeño pepper,** for serving

Helpful Hint

The most popular brand of sriracha—you know the one—is technically *not* vegan. (The sugar is processed with bone char, an animal by-product.) Luckily there are plenty of other brands that pass the vegan test!

6 Make the sandwich: Wipe out the skillet and return it to medium heat. Spread the butter on the cut sides of the baguettes. When the skillet is hot, press the buttered baguettes onto the surface and toast for about 2 minutes, until golden brown. Transfer the baguettes to two serving plates.

7 Add the vegetable oil to the skillet, again over medium heat. When the oil is shimmering, lay the marinated tofu slices in the skillet and fry for about 2 minutes on each side, until golden brown and warmed through.

8 Spread the spicy mayo on the toasted baguettes. Lay the tofu slices on the bottom halves of each sandwich, then layer on the cauliflower and the pickled carrot and radish. Finish with a sprinkle of cilantro and slices of cucumber and jalapeño, then gently press down on the top half of each baguette and serve.

Spaghetti-Ohs alla Vodka

2 tablespoons **olive oil**

1 small **shallot**, finely chopped

1 **garlic clove**, grated

1 (6-ounce) can **tomato paste**

2 tablespoons (1 ounce) **vodka**

1 cup **heavy cream**

½ teaspoon **red pepper flakes**

½ teaspoon **kosher salt**, plus more as needed

¼ teaspoon **freshly ground black pepper**

1 pound dried **anellini pasta**

2 tablespoons **unsalted butter**

Helpful Hint

Using pasta water in the sauce might seem odd, but trust us. The water is full of starch from the pasta, so it'll thicken the sauce to a perfectly creamy consistency. Just make sure to salt the pasta water thoroughly for excellent seasoning all around.

SpaghettiOs, a variety of canned ring-shaped pasta in tomato sauce, was introduced by Campbell's in 1965, and the phrase "uh-oh" was never the same again. The introduction of vodka sauce for pasta is a little harder to pin down. It was either invented in New York City by an Italian restaurateur in the 1970s or a by a Columbia University grad in the 1980s. Or maybe it was invented in Italy, at a restaurant in Bologna in the 1970s, or in Rome in the 1980s. But all that matters are two facts: vodka sauce is delicious and a round O shape is the most fun pasta ever. So, in a move of pure joy, we throw it all together in a dish everyone can enjoy.

1 In a large skillet, heat the olive oil over medium heat. When it begins to shimmer, add the shallot and cook, stirring occasionally, until softened, about 5 minutes. Add the garlic and cook 1 minute more, until fragrant. Stir in the tomato paste and cook until the paste is a deep red, about 5 minutes. Add the vodka and cook, stirring occasionally, until the liquid has mostly boiled off, about 3 minutes. Stir in the cream, red pepper flakes, salt, and pepper, then remove from the heat.

2 Bring a large pot of salted water to a boil over high heat. Cook the anellini until just al dente, according to the package directions. Reserve 1 cup of the pasta-cooking water before draining the pasta.

3 Add the anellini to the sauce and return the skillet to medium-high heat. Add the butter and ¼ cup of the pasta water. Stir constantly to coat the pasta with the sauce and to melt the butter. Taste for seasoning, and add enough more pasta water to achieve a smooth and creamy sauce.

4 Divide the pasta among four plates and serve immediately.

Gather Round

CHILI ACROSS THE COUNTRY

each serves 8

The origins of chili stretch all the way back to the Aztec empire (in present-day Mexico), as a stew seasoned with chiles. When northern Mexico became the state of Texas, a meaty red chili con carne became a major part of its culture. In contrast, New Mexico's traditional chili is a rich mixture of slow-cooked pork, tomatillos, and vibrant green chiles, giving it its signature verde. In the 1980s, California cuisine, with its emphasis on light eating and use of fresh ingredients, gave birth to the modern classic, white bean chili. But the winner for the most American chili has to be the one introduced by two Macedonian immigrants (a shout-out to Tom and John Kiradjieff!), who settled in Ohio in the early 1920s; Cincinnati chili is ground beef, heavily spiced with Mediterranean seasonings, served over spaghetti and topped with a truly creative array of kidney beans, shredded cheddar cheese, oyster crackers, and hot sauce.

Following are these four types of chili. No matter which you make or how you serve it, a pot of hot chili is the perfect excuse to gather round the table.

Cincinnati Chili

2 pounds **ground beef**

1 (8-ounce) can **tomato sauce**

1 (6-ounce) can **tomato paste**

1 large **white onion**, finely chopped

4 **garlic cloves**, minced

2 tablespoons **Worcestershire sauce**

2 tablespoons **kosher salt**

2 tablespoons **chili powder**

2 teaspoons **ground cumin**

1 teaspoon **ground cinnamon**

1 teaspoon **ground allspice**

½ teaspoon **cayenne pepper**

¼ teaspoon **ground cloves**

2 tablespoons **cocoa powder**

1 tablespoon **cider vinegar**

Warm cooked **spaghetti**; warmed, drained, and rinsed **red kidney beans**; shredded **cheddar cheese**; **oyster crackers**; and **hot sauce**, for serving

1 In a Dutch oven or large heavy pot, combine the beef with 4 cups of water. Use a wooden spoon to stir and break up the beef. Stir in the tomato sauce, tomato paste, onion, garlic, Worcestershire sauce, salt, chili powder, cumin, cinnamon, allspice, cayenne, and cloves.

2 Set the pot over high heat. As soon as the water starts simmering, reduce the heat to low. Simmer the chili, stirring occasionally, for at least 1 hour (but ideally 2 hours for maximum flavor and tenderness). Stir in the cocoa powder and vinegar, then serve the chili over spaghetti and top with the kidney beans and cheddar cheese. Serve with oyster crackers and hot sauce.

California White Bean Chili

1 tablespoon **olive oil**

1 medium **yellow onion**, finely chopped

2 **garlic cloves**, minced

1 teaspoon **dried oregano**

1 teaspoon **ground cumin**

1 (7-ounce) can **diced green chiles**

4 cups **chicken stock**

1 pound **boneless, skinless chicken breasts** or **thighs**, cut into 2-inch pieces

Kosher salt and **freshly ground black pepper**

2 (15-ounce) cans **cannellini beans**

1 cup **sour cream**

Chopped **fresh cilantro, shredded Monterey jack cheese**, sliced **avocado**, and crushed **tortilla chips**, for serving

1 In a Dutch oven or large heavy pot, heat the olive oil over medium heat. When the oil is shimmering, add the onion, garlic, oregano, and cumin and cook until the onion is softened, about 5 minutes. Add the chiles, including the liquid, and the stock and increase the heat to medium-high.

2 Season the chicken generously with salt and pepper. When the stock is simmering, use tongs to transfer the pieces to the pot. Simmer for about 10 minutes, until the chicken is just cooked through. Transfer the chicken to a cutting board to cool.

3 Add the cannellini beans, including the liquid, to the pot and reduce the heat to medium. Simmer for about 10 minutes, until the beans are heated through and soft. Use a wooden spoon to lightly mash about a third of the beans, then stir to activate the starch and thicken the soup. Remove from the heat.

4 Shred the chicken. Return it to the pot with any accumulated juices from the cutting board. Stir in the sour cream until just combined.

5 Divide the chili among bowls and serve with cilantro, cheese, avocado, and tortilla chips.

New Mexico Chili Verde

1 (16-ounce) can **lager beer** or **chicken stock**

1 pound **fresh tomatillos**, husked and rinsed

1 bunch **scallions**, trimmed

2 packed cups **fresh cilantro**, including leaves and stems, plus more for serving

4 **garlic cloves**

Kosher salt and freshly ground black pepper

2 tablespoons **olive oil**

2 **poblano** or **Anaheim chiles**, seeded and chopped

1 large **white onion**, finely chopped

4 pounds **boneless pork shoulder**, cut into 2-inch pieces

1 tablespoon **ground cumin**

1 tablespoon **dried oregano**

1 Add the beer, tomatillos, scallions, cilantro, garlic, 1 tablespoon salt, and 1 teaspoon pepper to a blender. Blend on high for about 1 minute to form a smooth salsa.

2 In a Dutch oven or large heavy pot, heat the olive oil over medium-high heat. When the oil is shimmering, add the chiles and onion and cook, stirring occasionally, until softened, about 5 minutes. Season the pork generously with salt and pepper, then add to the pot. Sear for about 2 minutes, until the bottom pieces are nicely browned, then stir, turning the pieces over, and sear for about 2 minutes more, until browned on the remaining sides. Stir in the cumin and oregano and cook for about 30 seconds, until fragrant.

3 Pour in the salsa from the blender. When the liquid starts to simmer, cover the pot, reduce the heat to medium-low, and simmer for about 2 hours, until the pork is falling apart.

4 Remove the pot from the heat and use a wooden spoon to gently break the pork into bite-sized pieces. Serve with additional chopped cilantro.

Texas Chili con Carne

2 ounces **dried ancho** or **guajillo chiles**

2 tablespoons **vegetable oil**

1 large **white onion**, finely chopped

2 pounds **boneless beef chuck**, cut into 1-inch pieces

Kosher salt and freshly ground black pepper

2 **garlic cloves**

2 packed tablespoons **dark brown sugar**

2 tablespoons **cider vinegar**

2 teaspoons **ground cumin**

4 cups **beef stock**

Sour cream and **lime** wedges, for serving

1 In a Dutch oven or large heavy pot, toast the chiles over medium heat until fragrant, 2 minutes per side. Transfer to a medium bowl and fill the bowl with hot water. Cover with plastic wrap and let soak for 15 minutes.

2 While the chiles soak, add the oil to the Dutch oven over medium heat. When the oil is shimmering, add the onion and cook, stirring occasionally, until softened, about 5 minutes. Season the beef with generous pinches of salt and pepper, then add it to the pot. Sear for about 2 minutes on each side until nicely browned all over. Remove the pot from the heat.

3 When the chiles are pliable, split them and remove the stems and seeds. (A pair of vinyl gloves comes in handy here!) Add the chiles to a blender along with the garlic, brown sugar, vinegar, cumin, the 2 teaspoons salt and 1 teaspoon pepper, then pour in the beef stock. Blend on high for about 1 minute to form a smooth salsa.

4 Pour the salsa into the pot with the beef. Return the pot to high heat and bring to a simmer. Cover the pot, reduce the heat to medium-low, and simmer for about 2 hours, until the beef is very tender.

5 Divide the chili among bowls and serve with the sour cream and lime wedges.

Eggplant Parm Casserole

Nonstick cooking spray

4 pounds **fresh eggplants**, cut lengthwise into ¼-inch-thick strips

6 tablespoons **olive oil**, plus more as needed

Kosher salt and **freshly ground black pepper**

1 cup **Italian-seasoned bread crumbs**

½ cup grated **Parmesan cheese**, plus more as needed

1 (24-ounce) jar **marinara sauce**

2 tablespoons **dried oregano**

1 tablespoon **fennel seeds**

½ teaspoon **red pepper flakes**

1 (15-ounce) container **whole milk ricotta**

2 cups shredded **mozzarella cheese** (see Note)

Chopped **fresh basil**, for serving

Helpful Hint

Pre-shredded cheese works great, but it is coated in additives to prevent clumping. Freshly shredded cheese is always the best bet for maximum melty goodness.

Melanzane alla parmigiana ("eggplant parm") originated in Southern Italy as a simple dish of fried eggplant baked with tomato sauce and cheese. To honor tradition, but up the ante on a warm plate of comfort, we merge the traditional preparation with the dense and gooey goodness of a lasagna. Slices of eggplant act as the pasta layers, but the marinara, stringy mozzarella, and globs of ricotta are still what you know and love. It's the ultimate "Why choose?" dinner.

1 Preheat the oven to 400°F and set racks in the center of the oven. Coat two rimmed baking sheets with nonstick spray.

2 Arrange the eggplant slices on the baking sheets (some overlap is okay). Drizzle each sheet with 2 tablespoons of the olive oil and generously season with salt and pepper. Bake for 30 minutes, rotating the pans halfway through, until the eggplant is soft.

3 In a small bowl, stir together the bread crumbs, Parmesan, remaining 2 tablespoons olive oil, and a generous pinch of salt.

4 In a medium bowl, stir together the marinara sauce, oregano, fennel seeds, and red pepper flakes.

5 Generously coat a 9 by 13-inch glass baking pan with nonstick spray. Spread ½ cup of the marinara sauce across the bottom of the pan. Use about one-fourth of the eggplant slices to create an even layer, overlapping the pieces as needed to cover the bottom. Dot 6 tablespoons of the ricotta over the eggplant. Repeat three times more with ½ cup each time of the sauce, then one-fourth of the eggplant and 6 tablespoons of the ricotta to create 4 layers in total. Cover the top with the remaining marinara sauce and sprinkle generously with the mozzarella.

6 Bake the lasagna for 20 to 25 minutes, until the mozzarella is melted and bubbly. Sprinkle the seasoned crumb mixture on top and return the dish to the oven to bake for about 10 minutes more, until golden brown. Let the lasagna rest for 15 minutes before slicing into 8 pieces. Place the pieces on individual plates and top each serving with the fresh basil, then serve.

Jamaican Jerk Pulled-Pork Sandwich

2 pounds **boneless pork shoulder**, cut into 1-inch pieces

Kosher salt and **freshly ground black pepper**

1 medium **yellow onion**, quartered

3 **scallions**, trimmed

2 **garlic cloves**

2 **Scotch bonnet** or habanero chiles

1 tablespoon **five-spice powder**

1 tablespoon **ground allspice**

1 teaspoon **dried thyme**

1 teaspoon **ground nutmeg**

½ cup **tamari** or **soy sauce**

8 **hamburger buns**, opened

Coleslaw (see page 113), for serving

Jamaican jerk seasoning emerged out of the shared traditions of the indigenous Taíno people and the Africans who escaped slavery to form free communities in the mountains of the island. Traditionally used to season a wild hog before slowly smoking it over an open fire, jerk seasoning has evolved as a popular rub and marinade for chicken, goat, or seafood cooked over a smoking jerk pit. For those of us who aren't lucky enough to have outdoor space, a slow roast in the oven gives the meat all the time it needs to develop deep layers of flavor and to reach a perfect tenderness. (A little tangy slaw and some soft burger buns don't hurt, either!)

1 Preheat the oven to 300°F and set a rack in the center.

2 Season the pork generously with salt and pepper and place in a Dutch oven or large, heavy oven-safe pot.

3 In a food processor or blender, combine the onion, scallions, garlic, chiles, five-spice powder, allspice, 1 tablespoon salt, 1 teaspoon black pepper, the thyme, and nutmeg. Pulse 6 to 8 times to create a thick paste. Add the tamari and then pulse 6 to 8 more times to create a thin paste.

4 Pour the jerk sauce over the pork. Set the pot over low heat and cook, stirring occasionally, until the pork has started to release some fat and the sauce is deeply fragrant, about 10 minutes. Cover and bake for about 1 hour, until the pork is tender. Remove the lid and continue to bake for 1 hour more, until the pork is very tender, almost falling apart.

5 Let the pork rest in the pot for 15 minutes. Reaching into the pot, use two forks to break apart and shred the meat.

6 Arrange the bottoms of the hamburger buns on serving plates. Divide the pork and its sauce among the bun bottoms and then top each with some coleslaw. Add the bun tops and serve.

Vegetable Tempura

2 quarts **vegetable oil**

FOR THE BATTER

2 large eggs

1 cup **seltzer**, chilled

1 cup **all-purpose flour**

FOR THE SAUCE

¼ cup **tamari** or **soy sauce**

¼ cup **mirin**

FOR THE VEGETABLES

½ small **acorn squash**, cut into small wedges, following the natural indents

1 medium **Japanese eggplant**, cut into ¼-inch rounds

1 medium **sweet potato**, cut into ¼-inch rounds

10 **fresh green beans**, ends trimmed

6 **fresh shiitake mushrooms**, stems removed

Flaky sea salt

Tempura—a deeply comforting dish of battered and fried seafood and vegetables—is a Japanese tradition that started with the arrival of Portuguese missionaries to Nagasaki. The Portuguese introduced a batter of eggs, water, and flour to coat seafood and vegetables during the Catholic fasting days, or Quattuor Témporas, which were observed four times a year. Japanese tempura continued to evolve as street food and was perfected in Tokyo in the 1800s, during the Edo period. (Fun fact: Other classic faves, like soba noodles and sushi, date to the same period!) Thanks to this long history of warm and crispy tempura, we have arguably the best solution for "eating your vegetables."

1 In a Dutch oven or large deep pot, heat the oil over medium-high heat. Use an instant-read thermometer to check periodically until the oil reaches 350°F.

2 Make the batter: In a medium bowl, whisk the eggs. Add the seltzer and flour, and whisk until just combined. (Some lumps are okay; don't overmix!)

3 Make the sauce: In a small bowl, whisk together the tamari and mirin.

4 Fry the vegetables: Add the cut pieces of acorn squash to the batter and toss to coat. Use tongs to transfer the batter-coated pieces to the hot oil and fry for about 3 minutes, until the coating is golden brown and the squash is tender. Transfer the squash to a plate lined with paper towels and sprinkle with some sea salt.

5 Working with one vegetable at a time, fry the eggplant, sweet potato, beans, and mushroom caps, first coating each with the batter and then dropping them into the hot oil to fry for about 3 minutes. Drain on the paper towels and sprinkle with some sea salt.

6 Arrange the fried vegetables on a large serving plate, with the bowl of dipping sauce in the center. Serve immediately.

Grape Jelly Meatballs

1 large egg

1 tablespoon **tomato paste**

1 tablespoon **Worcestershire sauce**

1 teaspoon **kosher salt**

½ teaspoon **freshly ground black pepper**

½ teaspoon **onion powder**

½ teaspoon **garlic powder**

1 pound **ground beef**

¼ cup **panko crumbs**

1 tablespoon **vegetable oil**

1 (12-ounce) jar **Heinz chili sauce**

1 (12-ounce) jar **grape jelly**

Helpful Hint

When mixing meatballs—any meatballs!—be careful not to overwork the mixture. A quick and gentle mix will yield light and moist meatballs.

Let's face it: The 1960s were a weird time in American food. The positive note was that more women than ever before were leaving their kitchens and joining the workforce. The negative was that packaged foods and an overemphasis on convenience were the new normal, especially when it came to entertaining. But here's the other positive: Not all of that packaged convenience was bad! If you've ever used a package of soup mix to make a dip or enjoyed a fondue, thank the '60s. And if you shudder at the thought of grape jelly meatballs, just consider how many times you've dunked chicken nuggets into a sweet-and-sour sauce. With a tart and sugary coating on these very savory meatballs, you'll find they're kind of addictive—and definitely delicious.

1 In a large bowl, whisk together the egg, tomato paste, Worcestershire sauce, salt, pepper, onion powder, and garlic powder. Add the ground beef and panko and use clean hands to gently blend into a cohesive mixture. Shape the mixture into 12 meatballs, about 1½ tablespoons each.

2 In a Dutch oven or large heavy pot, heat the oil over medium-high heat. Add the meatballs and fry until nicely browned, about 2 minutes per side.

3 While the meatballs fry, add the chili sauce and grape jelly to the bowl that contained the meatball mixture and whisk together. Pour the sauce over the browned meatballs and gently toss the meatballs to coat well. Bring to a simmer, cover the pot, reduce the heat to low, and cook for 1 hour, turning the meatballs over halfway through, until the meatballs are tender and the sauce is thickened. Serve immediately.

Tater Tot Hotdish

Nonstick cooking spray

1 tablespoon **olive oil**

2 pounds **ground turkey**

1 medium **yellow onion,**
  finely chopped

½ teaspoon **kosher salt**

¼ teaspoon **freshly ground**
  black pepper

2 (10.75-ounce) cans **condensed**
  cream of mushroom soup

2 cups **shredded cheddar**
  cheese

1 (32-ounce) package frozen
  Tater Tots

Finely chopped **fresh chives,**
  for serving

Hotdish casseroles are a firm Midwestern tradition, with recipes passed down through generations. The basic formula is to load a casserole dish with everything delicious, and the goal is to serve total comfort to a crowd at a family reunion, potluck dinner, or church supper. These are quick to throw together and are easy on the budget because they rely on some combination of canned concentrated soup, ground meat, grated cheese, and a starch like rice, pasta, or Tater Tots. We love the look of neatly lined-up tots on top, making this both comforting and cute!

1 Preheat the oven to 350°F and set a rack in the center. Thoroughly coat a 9 by 13-inch baking pan with nonstick spray.

2 In a large skillet, heat the oil over medium heat. When the oil is shimmering, add the ground turkey and onion. Cook, stirring and breaking up the meat with a wooden spoon, until the turkey is cooked through, 3 to 5 minutes.

3 Scoop the turkey and onion into a large bowl, leaving the fat in the pan behind. Season with the salt and pepper and stir to combine. Add the soup concentrate and stir again to blend the ingredients. Transfer to the prepared baking pan and then sprinkle on the shredded cheese.

4 Arrange the Tater Tots over the top in even rows. Bake the casserole for 30 to 35 minutes, until the Tater Tots are crisp and the casserole filling is bubbling. Finish with a sprinkling of the chives, then serve.

Aloo Gobi Soup

2 tablespoons **vegetable oil**

1 medium **red onion**, chopped

½ teaspoon **cumin seeds**

¼ teaspoon **fennel seeds**

¼ teaspoon **ground turmeric**

¼ teaspoon **cayenne pepper**

3 cups **fresh cauliflower florets** (from 1 head)

1 medium **russet potato**, peeled and diced into ½-inch pieces

1 (1-inch) piece **fresh ginger**, peeled and grated

2 **garlic cloves**, minced

1 **jalapeño pepper**, seeded and chopped

2 teaspoons **ground coriander**

1 teaspoon plus 1 tablespoon **kosher salt**

1 (14.5-ounce) can **diced tomatoes**, drained

Fresh cilantro leaves, for serving

Aloo gobi is a popular Indian and Pakistani dish of potatoes (aloo) and cauliflower (gobi), deeply seasoned with a variety of spices. We transferred all those comforting elements to a vegetarian soup that's as warm and satisfying as can be (and honestly puts other vegetable soups to shame). The recipe calls for water because when you're building this much flavor, the liquid practically makes itself. But if you have vegetable stock laying around, there's no harm in substituting that!

1 In a Dutch oven or large heavy pot, heat the oil over medium-high heat. When the oil is shimmering, add the red onion and cook, stirring occasionally, for about 5 minutes, until the onion starts to soften. Stir in the cumin seeds, fennel seeds, turmeric, and cayenne pepper and continue to cook for about 2 minutes, until the spices are fragrant.

2 Stir in the cauliflower, potato, ginger, garlic, jalapeño, coriander, and 1 teaspoon of the salt. Cook for about 2 minutes more, stirring to coat the vegetables in the spices. Add 4 cups of water and the remaining tablespoon salt, then bring to a simmer. Cover, reduce the heat to low, and simmer until the potatoes and cauliflower are tender, about 20 minutes.

3 Stir in the tomatoes, then ladle the soup into four bowls, sprinkle with the cilantro leaves, and serve immediately.

One-Pot Ground Beef Stroganoff

2 tablespoons **olive oil**

8 ounces **cremini mushrooms,** sliced

1 medium **white onion**, chopped

2 **garlic cloves**, minced

1 pound **ground beef**

1 tablespoon **smoked paprika**

1 tablespoon **kosher salt**

2 teaspoons **freshly ground black pepper**

¼ cup **dry sherry** (see Note)

4 cups **beef stock**

8 ounces **egg noodles**

1 tablespoon **cornstarch**

½ cup **sour cream**

Chopped **fresh parsley**, for serving

Named for a wealthy Russian aristocratic family (their name was Stroganoff, not Beef), this is a traditional dish that has traveled far and wide. You can find variations of it throughout Russia, northern Europe, and the UK, and as far away as Brazil, Japan, or Australia. And—of course—it is found in the United States, where it is a comfort-food classic. Each country has its unique twist on the basic, but we love the American tradition of curly egg noodles, a splash of alcohol, and a rich and creamy mushroom sauce. This version, whipped up all in one pot, is the ultimate in easy and delicious home cooking.

1 In a Dutch oven or large heavy pot, heat the oil over medium-high heat. When the oil is shimmering, add the mushrooms, onion, and garlic. Cook, stirring occasionally, until the onion and mushrooms are soft and starting to brown, about 8 minutes.

2 Add the ground beef, smoked paprika, salt, and pepper. Cook, using a wooden spoon to stir and break up the beef, until almost cooked through, about 5 minutes.

3 Add the sherry and simmer, scraping up any browned bits, until almost evaporated, about 3 minutes. Stir in the stock and add the noodles. Cover and reduce the heat to medium-low. Simmer for 10 to 15 minutes, until the noodles are al dente.

4 While the noodles cook, whisk the cornstarch and 1 tablespoon of water together in a small bowl until smooth, then whisk in the sour cream. When the noodles are done, stir the sour cream mixture into the pot and simmer for about 1 minute more, until slightly thickened.

5 Divide the stroganoff among four bowls and finish with a sprinkling of the parsley.

Note: No sherry? No problem! Substitute 2 tablespoons white wine vinegar mixed with 2 tablespoons water.

Chicken Piccata

Serves 4

1½ pounds **boneless, skinless chicken breasts**

2 teaspoons **kosher salt**

½ teaspoon **freshly ground black pepper**

½ cup **all-purpose flour**

3 tablespoons **vegetable oil,** plus more as needed

1 **shallot,** finely minced

1 **garlic clove,** finely minced

¼ cup **dry white wine** (see Note)

½ cup **chicken stock**

½ **fresh lemon,** thinly sliced

1 tablespoon drained **capers**

4 tablespoons (½ stick) **unsalted butter,** cold

Finely chopped **fresh parsley,** for serving

Helpful Hint

There's always a possibility that wine (or any other alcohol) could briefly flame up in the hot pan. Don't ever pour directly from the bottle, and make sure you step back a bit before adding it. For safety's sake!

Piccata is an Italian dish, traditionally prepared with veal cutlet or a swordfish fillet. But just as with many traditional dishes that arrive in the United States, the recipe was adapted by Italian immigrants to meet American palates and to satisfy our growing hunger for chicken. Thinly pounded chicken breasts are dredged and fried, then all that chicken-y fond (the delicious brown bits at the bottom of the skillet) becomes the base for a perfectly balanced lemon sauce. Buttery, acidic, briny, and fresh, chicken piccata is total comfort at its finest.

1 Slice the chicken breasts in half horizontally to create thinner pieces. Place the chicken cutlets between two pieces of plastic wrap and lightly pound with a cast-iron skillet or wooden spoon to create an even ½-inch thickness. Place the chicken cutlets in a medium bowl and season with the salt and pepper. Let rest for 15 minutes.

2 Place the flour in a wide, shallow bowl. Dip each chicken cutlet in the flour, lightly coating both sides, then shake off the excess. Set the coated chicken cutlets on a large plate.

3 In a large skillet, heat 2 tablespoons of the oil over medium-high heat. Working in two batches, add the chicken cutlets in a single layer. Fry undisturbed for 2 to 3 minutes, until golden brown, then flip and cook for about 1 minute, until the other side is lightly browned. (The chicken will not be fully cooked through at this point.) Add more oil between batches as needed.

4 Add the remaining tablespoon oil to the skillet along with the shallot. Cook, scraping up any browned bits, for about 2 minutes until the shallot is soft. Stir in the garlic, then add the wine, stock, lemon slices, and capers. Simmer for about 2 minutes, until the liquid is reduced by one-third. Add the chicken cutlets to the skillet and continue to simmer until the chicken is cooked through and the sauce has thickened, about 2 minutes more.

5 Transfer the chicken to a serving platter. Remove the skillet from the heat and whisk in the butter to form a smooth and silky sauce. Pour over the chicken and garnish with the parsley before serving.

Note: Feel free to substitute the wine with 2 tablespoons white wine vinegar mixed with 2 tablespoons water.

Extra-Cheesy French Onion Soup

4 tablespoons **olive oil**

2 tablespoons **unsalted butter**

3 large **Vidalia onions**, peeled, cut in half, and thinly sliced

2 teaspoons **kosher salt**

½ teaspoon **freshly ground black pepper**, plus more for serving

½ teaspoon **sugar**

1 cup **dry white wine** or **chicken stock**

4 cups **beef stock**

5 sprigs **fresh thyme**

2 **dried bay leaves**

1 **demi baguette** or ½ **baguette**, cut into 1-inch rounds

1 **garlic clove**, cut in half

8 ounces **Gruyère cheese**, grated

1 tablespoon **sherry** or **cognac** (optional)

French onion soup originated in Paris in the 1700s, but it became popular in New York City in 1861, when chef Marie Julie Grandjean Mouquin (what a name!) started making the soup in the kitchen of her husband's restaurant. Sweet from the onions, savory from the beef stock, cheesey from the, well, cheese, it's the perfect bowl of comfort. And if you've ever wondered why there's bread floating on top, here's the quick alphabet soup on that: The English word soup comes from the French word soupe, which comes from the Latin word suppa, which comes from the early German word supô, which describes a piece of bread that is soaked in broth before eating. How's that for a full circle?

1 In a large pot, heat the olive oil and butter over medium-low heat. When the butter is melted, stir in the onions. Cover and cook for about 20 minutes, until the onions are soft. Increase the heat to medium-high and add 1 teaspoon of the salt, plus the ½ teaspoon pepper and the sugar. Continue cooking and stirring until the onions are golden brown and caramelized, about 20 minutes.

2 Add the wine and scrape up all the browned bits on the bottom of the pot. Continue simmering and stirring until the wine has evaporated, about 10 minutes. Add the stock, thyme, bay leaves, and remaining teaspoon salt. Bring to a boil, then reduce the heat to medium-low and simmer for about 30 minutes, until the soup is thick and flavorful.

3 While the soup simmers, set the broiler to high and set a rack in the upper third of the oven. Place the baguette slices on a rimmed baking sheet and toast for about 1 minute, until crisp. Flip the slices and toast the other side for about 1 minute more. Rub the garlic clove on each side of the toasted bread. Sprinkle half the cheese evenly over the bread, then return the slices to the broiler once more. Toast for 1 to 2 minutes, until the cheese is melted.

4 Stir the sherry into the soup. Ladle the soup into four bowls, filling each about halfway. Sprinkle the remaining cheese over the soup and then float 2 pieces of the cheesy toast in each soup bowl. Top with grinds of black pepper and serve.

Helpful Hint

Making a bouquet garni (roughly translated, "a bouquet of deliciousness") of your herbs is an easy way to fish out the sprigs of thyme or the bay leaves after cooking. Simply gather the herbs in a bundle and tie them tightly together with a piece of string. When it's time for them to leave the broth, you can use a spoon to pull the bouquet out all at once.

Potato & Cheese Pierogi with Caramelized Onions

FOR THE ONIONS

4 large **yellow onions**, cut in half and thinly sliced

2 tablespoons **olive oil**

½ teaspoon **kosher salt**

½ teaspoon **freshly ground black pepper**

¼ cup **dry white wine** or **chicken stock**

FOR THE PIEROGI

4½ cups **all-purpose flour**, plus more as needed

3 tablespoons **olive oil**

3 **large egg**

1¼ cups **sour cream**, plus more for serving

1 pound **russet potatoes**, peeled and cut in half

½ cup shredded **Gruyère cheese**

1 teaspoon **kosher salt**, plus more as needed

1 teaspoon **freshly ground black pepper**, plus more as needed

2 tablespoons **unsalted butter**

Finely chopped **fresh chives**, for serving

Pierogi in Polish simply means "filled dumplings." Almost every culture in the world has some form of dumpling, whether it's stuffed, like Tibetan momo, Italian ravioli, or Chilean empanadas, or it's steamed, like Israeli matzo balls, South African dombolo, or American chicken and dumplings. In Eastern and Central Europe, pierogi come by many names and just as many fillings. Here we stick to the total-comfort basics: potato, cheese, caramelized onions, and plenty of sour cream. Smacznego!

1 Make the onions: In a large skillet, toss the onions with the olive oil, salt, and pepper. Set the skillet over medium heat and, stirring occasionally, cook until the onions start to sizzle. Continue to cook, stirring occasionally, until the onions are lightly golden, about 15 minutes. Add the wine and continue cooking and stirring until the onions are golden brown and soft as jam, about 15 minutes more. Remove the skillet from the heat.

2 Make the pierogi: In a medium bowl, stir together the flour, olive oil, egg, and 1 cup of the sour cream. When the dough comes together, knead it in the bowl for about 3 minutes, until smooth. Place the dough on a piece of plastic wrap and flatten into a disc. Wrap tightly with the plastic and refrigerate while making the filling.

3 Add the potatoes to a large pot and fill with cold water. Cover the pot and set over high heat. Bring to a boil, then boil the potatoes for about 20 minutes, until they are fork-tender.

4 Drain the potatoes and rinse under cold water. Place them in a large bowl and add the cheese, 1 teaspoon salt, 1 teaspoon pepper, and the remaining ¼ cup sour cream. Mash everything together to form a cohesive mixture.

5 Lightly flour a work surface. Unwrap the dough, lightly flour the top, and roll it out to about a ⅛-inch thickness. Use a pint glass to cut out 3-inch circles. Gather the scraps, re-roll, and continue cutting until you have 20 circles.

6 Scoop a tablespoon of the filling into the center of each circle. Stretch the dough to fold it in half and then tightly pinch the edges of the dough closed.

recipe continues

7 Bring a large pot of salted water to a boil. Working in batches, drop the pierogi in the water and boil for about 3 minutes, until they float to the surface. Use a spider strainer to scoop the pierogi out of the pot and transfer them to the skillet with the caramelized onions.

8 When all the pierogies are cooked, place the skillet over medium heat and add the butter. Gently shake the skillet to toss the pierogies and onions in the butter. Continue to cook for about 2 minutes, until the onions are sizzling.

9 Transfer the pierogi and onions to a serving platter and garnish with chives. Serve with plenty of sour cream.

Shrimp Pad Thai

8 ounces **wide rice noodles**

¼ cup **palm sugar** or **light brown sugar**

¼ cup **Thai fish sauce**

¼ cup **tamarind paste**

1 tablespoon **vegetable oil**

8 ounces **large shrimp**, peeled and deveined

1 (4-ounce) piece **extra-firm tofu**, cubed

2 **garlic cloves**, minced

2 **shallots**, minced

1 **large egg**

4 **scallions**, white and green parts sliced into 1-inch pieces, plus more for serving

½ cup **mung bean sprouts**, plus more for serving

Lime wedges and chopped **peanuts**, for serving

Helpful Hint

A pink and curled-up shrimp is probably cooked through, but check the slice along the shrimp's back where the vein was removed. If it's solid white with no translucent areas, the shrimp are good to go!

Pad Thai has a debatable history, but we know for sure it's a fairly new dish in Thai cuisine, introduced sometime around the 1930s. One theory is that Prime Minister Phibunsongkhram introduced it as a national dish to unite the country; other theories are based on the use of rice noodles as a way to deal with food rationing during World War II. No matter how it originated, one thing we can all agree on is that Pad Thai is at the top of the list of total-comfort foods. With a sauce that's only three ingredients but surprisingly deep in flavor, and a quick preparation that's made in one skillet, this recipe is the best reason to *not* order delivery tonight.

1 Add the rice noodles to a medium bowl and fill with warm water. Soak for 30 minutes, then drain.

2 In a small saucepan, whisk together the palm sugar, fish sauce, and tamarind paste over medium-high heat. Bring to a boil, reduce the heat, and simmer for about 5 minutes, until the sauce is reduced to ½ cup. Remove from the heat.

3 In a large skillet, heat the oil over high heat. When the oil is shimmering, add the shrimp and tofu. Cook for about 2 minutes, then flip the shrimp and tofu over and cook for about 1 minute more, until the shrimp is opaque and the tofu has taken on some color. Stir in the garlic and shallots, then use a wooden spoon to push everything to one side of the skillet.

4 Add the egg to the skillet and use the wooden spoon to scramble it, about 30 seconds. Stir in the noodles, the chopped 4 scallions and ½ cup bean sprouts, and the reduced sauce. Stir to thoroughly blend everything well, then remove the skillet from the heat.

5 Divide the pad Thai between two serving plates and accompany with a lime wedge, more scallions and bean sprouts, and a sprinkling of the chopped peanuts.

Surf & Turf Sliders

1 (8-ounce) container **crab meat or package imitation crab meat**, shredded or chopped into ¼-inch pieces

2 tablespoons **mayonnaise**

1 tablespoon finely chopped **fresh chives**

1 teaspoon **fresh lemon juice**

1 pound **ground beef**

1 tablespoon **Old Bay** seasoning

12 **slider buns**

1 tablespoon **vegetable oil**

12 **large shrimp**, peeled, deveined, and cooked

We covered the culinary pros and cons of the 1960s (see Grape Jelly Meatballs on page 93), but another huge pro of that era is the popular surf 'n' turf. The trend of serving lobster and steak together actually started in the late 1800s, but quickly fell out of fashion. When it came swinging back in the 1960s, this time it stuck around. The "turf" is almost always beef, but the "surf" can range from lobster to crab legs to shrimp. For this burger, we pulled in the best of everything, for a juicy slider flavored with Old Bay seasoning, some lemony crab salad piled on top, and shrimp as a delicious garnish.

1 In a medium bowl, stir together the crab, mayonnaise, chives, and lemon juice. Cover with plastic wrap and refrigerate.

2 In another medium bowl, use clean hands to mix the beef and the seasoning. Divide the meat into 12 equal balls. Arrange the bottom halves of the buns on a serving plate.

3 In a large skillet, heat the oil over medium heat. When the oil is shimmering, add half the meatballs, then use a spatula to gently press them flat into patties. Sear for about 2 minutes, until the bottoms are crisp. Flip over and sear for about 2 minutes more on the other sides for medium or 4 minutes for well done. Transfer the burgers to the bun halves on the serving plate, then cook the remaining meatballs and flatten into patties, then place on remaining bun halves.

4 Spoon the crab mixture on top of the burgers, then place the bun tops on the sliders. Position a shrimp on top of each slider and coax a toothpick through to hold everything in place. Serve immediately.

Something on the Side

TIMELESS PICNIC SALADS each serves 8

There are lots of excellent side dishes (see the rest of this chapter), but when you're eating outdoors, there are four salads that are must-haves: macaroni, potato, coleslaw, and bean. Everyone has their special twists on the classics, but these four regional variations are worth a try. Hawaiian macaroni salad originally appeared as part of the plate lunches (a cousin of the Japanese bento box) served to day laborers on the islands while under early American occupation and influence. Three bean salad mostly likely has its origins in balela, a Middle Eastern salad of chickpeas, black beans, tomatoes, and herbs. Coleslaw came to America via the Dutch koolsla, a simple mixture of vinegar, oil, and cabbage; and while people in some areas of the United States (like in North Carolina) stick close to the original, others (like in Tennessee) prefer it with creamy mayonnaise. And finally, potato salad, which originated in Germany, came to America with the Pennsylvania Dutch, who earned their name from a misunderstanding of the German word for "German": Deutsch. Think of these four recipes as the foundation for boosting your own picnic traditions to new heights.

Hawaiian Macaroni Salad

1 (1-pound) box **elbow macaroni**

2 cups **mayonnaise**

2 tablespoons **cider vinegar**

1 tablespoon **onion powder**

1 tablespoon **sugar**

1 teaspoon **kosher salt**

2 cups shredded **carrots**

4 **scallions**, white and green parts thinly sliced

¼ cup **buttermilk**

1 Bring a large pot of salted water to a boil over high heat. Add the macaroni and cook until al dente, according to the package directions.

2 In a large bowl, whisk together the mayonnaise, vinegar, onion powder, sugar, and salt.

3 Drain the pasta and add to the bowl with the mayonnaise mixture. Let cool completely, about 30 minutes (or up to 24 hours). Just before serving, fold in the carrots, scallions, and buttermilk.

Southwestern Three Bean Salad

1 medium **red onion**, finely chopped

2 tablespoons **red wine vinegar**

1 (15.5-ounce) can **red kidney beans**, drained and rinsed

1 (15.5-ounce) can **black beans**, drained and rinsed

1 (15.5-ounce) can **chickpeas**, drained and rinsed

1 (15.5-ounce) jar **thick and chunky salsa**

2 **celery stalks**, thinly sliced

2 cups **fresh** or thawed **frozen corn kernels**

1 tablespoon **Sazón** seasoning with coriander and annatto

1 teaspoon **kosher salt**

1 In a large bowl, toss together the red onion and vinegar. Let marinate for about 5 minutes until the onion is vibrantly red.

2 Add the kidney beans, black beans, chickpeas, salsa, celery, corn, seasoning, and salt to the bowl with the onions. Toss to fully incorporate, cover, and refrigerate for at least 1 hour or up to 24 hours before serving.

Creamy Memphis Coleslaw

2 cups **mayonnaise**

2 tablespoons **dry mustard**

2 tablespoons **cider vinegar**

1 tablespoon **sugar**

2 teaspoons **celery salt**

1 teaspoon **onion powder**

2 (16-ounce) bags **coleslaw mix**

1 In a large bowl, whisk together the mayonnaise, dry mustard, vinegar, sugar, celery salt, and onion powder.

2 Add the coleslaw mix and toss to combine. Cover and refrigerate for at least 1 hour or up to 24 hours before serving.

Pennsylvania Dutch Potato Salad

4 large **eggs**

2 pounds **russet potatoes**, cut into 1-inch cubes

1 medium **red onion**, finely chopped

2 tablespoons **sugar**

2 tablespoons **cider vinegar**

2 tablespoons **Dijon mustard**

1 teaspoon **salt**

1 teaspoon **freshly ground black pepper**

4 **celery stalks**, thinly sliced

1 cup **mayonnaise**

1 Bring a large pot of salted water to a boil over high heat. Fill a medium bowl with ice water.

2 Use a slotted spoon to gently lower the eggs into the boiling water. Boil for 10 minutes, then immediately transfer to the ice water. As soon as the water starts boiling again, add the potatoes. Boil for about 20 minutes, until fork-tender.

3 In a large bowl, combine the red onion, sugar, vinegar, mustard, salt, and pepper. Crack, peel, and rinse the hard-boiled eggs. Cut the eggs into quarters.

4 Drain the potatoes thoroughly and add to the bowl with the onion mixture. Toss to thoroughly coat the potatoes, then add the celery and mayonnaise and toss again. Gently fold in the eggs, being careful not to break the pieces. Cover and refrigerate for at least 1 hour or up to 24 hours before serving.

Extra-Dilly Fried Pickles

FOR THE SAUCE

1 cup **mayonnaise**

1 teaspoon **Old Bay** seasoning

FOR THE PICKLES

1 (16-ounce) jar **sliced dill pickles**

½ cup **all-purpose flour**

1 teaspoon **dried dill**

1 teaspoon **baking powder**

1 teaspoon **kosher salt**

¼ teaspoon **cayenne pepper**

2 quarts **vegetable oil**

Flaky sea salt

Helpful Hint

Flaky sea salt is a smart move on fried foods. It adds an extra crunchy texture and the perfect seasoning boost for every bite.

As with most fried things, we can trace these fried pickles to the U.S. South. Many credit Bernell "Fatman" Austin for popularizing fried pickles at his Arkansas drive-in restaurant in 1963. But what started as a regional specialty quickly became a staple of county fairs, diners, and chain restaurants nationwide. A simple dipping sauce of mayo and Old Bay adds the perfect accent, while the batter for the pickles offers an extra boost of dill and a burst of pickle juice. These fried pickles are crispy, crunchy, and unbelievably good.

1 Make the sauce: In a small bowl, whisk together the mayonnaise and seasoning. Cover with plastic wrap and refrigerate until ready to serve.

2 Make the pickles: Set a fine-mesh strainer over a medium bowl. Pour the pickles into the strainer, retaining the brine in the bowl. Set aside to drain completely.

3 In a large bowl, whisk together the flour, dill, baking powder, salt, and cayenne. Measure ½ cup of the reserved pickle brine and whisk it into the flour mixture. (Pour the remaining pickle brine back into the jar and reserve for another use.)

4 Add the pickles to the batter and use a rubber spatula to stir and coat them thoroughly. Set aside for about 10 minutes, until the batter has thickened.

5 In a Dutch oven or large heavy pot, heat the oil over medium-high heat. Use an instant-read thermometer to check periodically until the oil hits 350°F.

6 Use tongs to transfer about half the batter-coated pickles to the oil. (It's okay if some of the pickles are stuck together.) Fry until golden brown, 2 to 3 minutes, then transfer to a plate lined with paper towels. Sprinkle the hot pickles with the flaky sea salt. Fry the remaining pickles, then drain and sprinkle with salt. Serve immediately, with the chilled dipping sauce.

Creole Red Beans & Rice

2 slices **thick-cut bacon,** chopped

2 **andouille sausages,** cut in half and cut into ½-inch pieces

1 **white onion,** diced

1 **celery stalk,** diced

1 **green bell pepper,** cored, seeded, and diced

4 **garlic cloves,** minced

1 **dried bay leaf**

1 tablespoon **smoked paprika**

1 teaspoon **kosher salt**

½ teaspoon **dried thyme**

¼ teaspoon **cayenne pepper**

2 cups **chicken stock**

1 (15.5-ounce) can **red kidney beans**

1 tablespoon **red wine vinegar**

2 cups cooked **white rice**

Scallions, white and green parts thinly sliced, and **hot sauce,** for serving

Traditionally made on Mondays with leftover meat from Sunday, seasoned with the "holy trinity" (bell pepper, onion, and celery), and left to simmer on the stove all day, a Creole bowl of red beans and rice is total comfort in every sense. Creole cuisine was born from a mix of French and Spanish colonizers, Native Americans, enslaved and freed Africans, Haitian immigrants, plus marriages intermingling Irish, Italian, and German immigrants. Red beans and rice is still a staple of Louisiana Creole food, and one of the best examples of the love, care, and resilience that goes into classic home cooking.

1 In a medium saucepan, add the bacon and set over medium heat. Cook, stirring occasionally, until the fat has rendered and the bacon is starting to crisp, about 5 minutes. Add the andouille and continue to cook until the sausage is starting to brown, about 5 minutes more. Use a slotted spoon to transfer the meat to a small bowl, leaving the fat in the pan.

2 Add the onion, celery, and bell pepper to the pan. Cook, stirring occasionally, until the vegetables are soft and fragrant, about 5 minutes. Stir in the garlic, bay leaf, smoked paprika, salt, thyme, and cayenne. Cook for about 1 minute more, until the spices are fragrant.

3 Add the stock and bring to a simmer. Cook the mixture for about 10 minutes, until reduced by half. Add the bacon and sausage, plus the kidney beans and their liquid. Simmer for about 5 minutes more, until the beans are warmed through and the sauce is thickened. Remove from the heat and stir in the vinegar. Taste for seasoning.

4 Divide the rice between four bowls and spoon the red beans and liquid over the rice. Serve with a sprinkle of scallions and plenty of hot sauce.

Twice-Baked Potato Croquettes

FOR THE POTATOES

1½ pounds **russet potatoes,** scrubbed

2 tablespoons **olive oil**

Kosher salt and **freshly ground black pepper**

FOR THE CROQUETTES

4 slices **cooked bacon,** crumbled

2 cups **shredded cheddar cheese**

3 **scallions**, white and green parts thinly sliced

1 teaspoon **freshly ground black pepper**

3 teaspoons **kosher salt**

1 cup **all-purpose flour**

2 large **eggs**

2 cups **panko crumbs**

2 tablespoons **olive oil**

Sour cream, for serving

Helpful Hint

Baking the potatoes in the microwave?! Believe it or not, it's the fastest and best way to get an evenly baked potato. If the microwave isn't an option, though, wrap the potatoes in foil and bake at 350°F for 1 hour.

Croquettes, or some variation on them, are found in many cuisines around the world. Here, we use a twice-baked potato as inspo for a turbo-charged croquette. The potatoes get mashed with bacon, cheese, scallions—you know, everything good—then coated in panko and baked until perfectly crisp. It's total comfort with every bite!

1 Make the potatoes: Prick the potatoes all over with a fork to create shallow holes. Rub the skins with the olive oil and season well with salt and pepper. Place on a microwave-safe dish and microwave for about 7 minutes, using tongs to flip the potatoes halfway through. Test the potatoes for doneness, then continue to microwave in 2-minute increments until soft. You'll know they're cooked through when a knife easily slides through the potato and back out. Cut the potatoes in half crosswise and set aside to cool, about 20 minutes.

2 Make the croquettes: Preheat the oven to 400°F and set a rack in the center. Line a rimmed baking sheet with foil.

3 Set aside about 1 tablespoon each of the bacon, cheese, and scallions for serving. In a large bowl, combine the remaining bacon, cheese, and scallions, then add the pepper and 2 teaspoons salt.

4 In a shallow bowl, whisk together the flour and ½ teaspoon salt. In a second shallow bowl, whisk together the eggs and ½ teaspoon salt. In a third shallow bowl, mix the panko and olive oil.

5 Roughly chop the cooled potatoes and add to the large bowl. Use a large spoon to mash the potatoes and blend with the other ingredients in the bowl.

6 Scoop a heaping tablespoon of the potato mixture and use your hands to shape it into a cylinder. Toss the croquette in the flour to coat well, then dip in the beaten egg and let the excess drip off. Finally, roll the croquette in the bread crumbs to coat completely. Transfer the croquette to the prepared baking sheet, then shape, dip, and coat the remaining potato mixture.

7 Make sure the croquettes have 1 inch of space between them on the baking sheet. Bake for 12 to 15 minutes, until golden brown.

8 Place the croquettes on a large serving platter. Sprinkle on the reserved bacon, cheese, and scallions, then finish with a dollop of sour cream. Serve immediately.

Bacon-Wrapped Green Beans

1 pound whole **fresh green beans**, ends trimmed

8 slices **thick-cut bacon**

2 tablespoons **olive oil**

1 teaspoon **kosher salt**

½ teaspoon **garlic powder**

1 tablespoon finely chopped **fresh rosemary**

1 tablespoon **dark brown sugar**

A classic of Southern home cooking, where even the vegetables have bacon! But this time the bacon serves a purpose, acting as the perfect little tie for adorable green beans bundles, making them maybe the most elegant vegetable side ever. After a few bites into those bundles—perfectly tender, salty, and slathered with a rosemary-brown sugar mixture—you'll start to wonder: Should everything have bacon? It's a question worth exploring.

1 Preheat the oven to 400°F and set a rack in the center. Line a rimmed baking sheet with foil.

2 Bring a large pot of salted water to a boil. Add the beans and boil for 1 minute, until vibrant green. Drain and immediately rinse under cold water to stop the cooking. Transfer the green beans to a kitchen towel and pat dry.

3 Lay the bacon in an even layer on the baking sheet. Bake for about 10 minutes, until the bacon is taking some color but is still soft and pliable. Transfer the bacon to a plate lined with paper towels to drain and set the baking sheet aside.

4 In a medium bowl, whisk together the olive oil, salt, and garlic powder. Add the green beans and toss to thoroughly coat the beans with the seasoning.

5 In a small bowl, whisk together the rosemary and brown sugar with 1 tablespoon of water.

6 Gather the beans in bundles of 10. Wrap each bundle in a piece of bacon and secure with a toothpick. Arrange the bundles on the baking sheet and spoon the rosemary mixture over the tops. Bake the wrapped beans for 15 to 20 minutes, until the bacon is crisp and the green beans are tender. Remove the toothpicks and arrange the bundles on a serving plate.

Broccoli with Vegan Cheese Sauce

1 tablespoon **olive oil**

½ small **white onion**, finely chopped

1 **garlic clove**, minced

1 small **russet potato**, peeled and cut into ½-inch cubes

1 small **carrot**, cut into ¼-inch-thick coins

¼ cup **raw cashews**

3 tablespoons **nutritional yeast**

1 tablespoon **white miso**

1 teaspoon **Dijon mustard**

½ teaspoon **ground turmeric**

1 teaspoon **kosher salt**, plus more as needed

6½ cups **fresh broccoli florets** (from 2 crowns)

Helpful Hint
Avoid that old plate of mushy, drab broccoli. Retrieve a piece of broccoli from the pot as it cooks and run it under cold water, then take a bite. It should still have a little crunch but give in easily—what we call crisp-tender.

One of the most nostalgic of childhood side dishes, there's no arguing that broccoli bathed in cheese sauce is an absolute delicacy. But for those of us who want a little *more* vegetable with our vegetable, this vegan cheese sauce is the perfect solution. We toss out the dairy but keep all the silky richness of melted cheese by employing a secret arsenal of carrots, potatoes, and cashews. A quick boil and blend are all it takes to produce a delicious sauce that will fool the young and young at heart alike.

1 In a large saucepan, heat the olive oil over medium heat until shimmering. Add the onion and cook, stirring occasionally, until it is starting to become translucent, about 8 minutes. Stir in the garlic and continue to cook until deeply fragrant, about 2 minutes more. Add the potato, carrot, cashews, and 2 cups of water to the saucepan. Increase the heat to high and bring the liquid to a boil. Reduce the heat to medium and simmer until the potato and carrot are very soft and the cashews are swollen, 10 to 15 minutes. Remove from the heat and let cool for 10 minutes.

2 Carefully pour the vegetables and liquid into a blender. Add the nutritional yeast, miso, mustard, turmeric, and 1 teaspoon salt. Blend on high speed for 1 to 2 minutes, until the mixture is smooth. Pour into a bowl and taste for salt, adding more if needed. Cover with plastic wrap.

3 Bring a large pot of salted water to a boil. Add the broccoli and boil for about 3 minutes, until vibrant green and crisp-tender. Drain the broccoli and arrange on a serving platter. Spoon the cheese sauce over the florets and serve immediately.

Ghanaian Jollof Rice

2½ cups **long-grain rice**

2 large **yellow onions**, roughly chopped

¼ cup plus 2 tablespoons **vegetable oil**

1 (28-ounce) can **whole peeled tomatoes**

1 (6-ounce) can **tomato paste**

1 or 2 **habanero chiles**

2 teaspoons **curry powder**

1 teaspoon **garlic powder**

1 teaspoon **ground ginger**

1 teaspoon **dried oregano**

1 teaspoon **kosher salt**

3 **chicken** or **vegetarian bouillon cubes**

1 cup **frozen mixed vegetables**

Helpful Hint

Thick tomato sauce can bubble and splatter everywhere. Invest in a cheap splatter guard to hold the mess back or place a lid partly over the pot, leaving about a fourth of the simmering surface exposed so steam can escape.

Jollof rice is one of the most important dishes of West African cooking, a centerpiece at gatherings to eat, share, celebrate, and love. The name may vary—zaamè in Mali, ceebu jën or benachin in Senegal and Gambia, sometimes riz au gras in French-speaking regions—but this dish of heavily seasoned and slowly cooked rice is a great multicultural connector. In fact, every West African country has a variation on the dish and every West African country believes theirs is the best. (Diplomatic answer: They're all correct.) And for the record, we're not taking sides with this recipe; it's just the perfect place to begin your jollof education. But one thing every home cook in every country can agree on: Jollof is always best when made the night before, refrigerated, and warmed up the next day.

1 Place the rice in a fine-mesh strainer and rinse under cold water, swirling with your fingers, until the water runs clear.

2 Add the onions and 2 tablespoons of the oil to a blender or food processor and blend until smooth, about 1 minute. Transfer to a medium bowl.

3 Add the whole tomatoes with their liquid, tomato paste, chiles, curry powder, garlic powder, ginger, oregano, salt, and bouillon cubes to the blender or food processor and blend until smooth, about 1 minute.

4 In a Dutch oven or large heavy pot, heat the remaining ¼ cup oil over medium heat. When the oil is shimmering, add the onion puree. Cook, stirring occasionally, until the puree has thickened and is starting to brown, about 10 minutes.

5 Stir in the tomato puree and reduce the heat to low. Cook for 30 to 40 minutes, stirring occasionally, until the stew has reduced by half and is a deep red (see Note).

6 Increase the heat to medium-high and add the drained rice, the frozen vegetables, and 1½ cups of water. Stir well and bring to a boil. Cover, reduce the heat to low, and simmer for about 30 minutes, stirring well every 10 minutes, until the rice is tender and the liquid is absorbed.

7 Divide the rice among bowls and serve immediately. Alternatively, let the pot of rice come to room temperature, then cover and refrigerate overnight. Before serving, set the covered pot over low heat for 15 to 20 minutes until the rice is warm.

Smoky Zaalouk Dip

FOR THE EGGPLANT

2 medium **eggplants**

3 tablespoons **vegetable oil**

FOR THE DIP

4 large **ripe tomatoes**

1 tablespoon **olive oil**, plus more
for serving

4 **garlic cloves**, grated

2 tablespoons chopped **fresh
parsley**, plus more for serving

2 tablespoons chopped **fresh
cilantro**, plus more for serving

2 teaspoons **ground cumin**

2 teaspoons **smoked paprika**

1½ teaspoons **kosher salt**, plus
more as needed

1 tablespoon **fresh lemon juice**

Chopped **pistachios**, for serving

Moroccan khobz or warmed
pita, for dipping

Spreads, salads, and dips featuring eggplant are a staple in
the Mediterranean countries of the Middle East, North Africa,
and southern Europe, with baba ghanoush or moutabel as two
well-known examples. Zaaalouk, a popular Moroccan dish,
is no exception. On the surface it seems like a simple combo
of eggplant and tomato, but the balance of herbs, spices,
crunchy pistachios, and smoky char gives it layers of flavors
that will have everyone diving in, bite after bite. Equally great
warm or cold, it's the perfect go-to dip for all occasions.

1 Make the eggplant: Preheat the broiler to high. Line a rimmed
baking sheet with foil and rub with 1 tablespoon of the oil.

2 Trim the eggplants, then cut in half lengthwise. Rub the eggplants
all over with the remaining 2 tablespoons oil and place cut side
down on the prepared baking sheet. Broil the eggplants for about
20 minutes, until the skins are charred and the flesh is tender.
Remove from the oven and let cool.

3 Make the dip: Slice the tomatoes in half and use a spoon to scrape
out the seeds. Roughly chop the tomatoes.

4 In a large saucepan, heat the olive oil over medium heat. When
the oil is shimmering, add the chopped tomatoes, the garlic,
2 tablespoons parsley, 2 tablespoons cilantro, the cumin, smoked
paprika, and a good pinch of salt. Cover and simmer, stirring
occasionally, until the tomatoes are broken down, about 15 minutes.
Remove the lid and continue to simmer, stirring often, until the
sauce thickens, about 5 minutes more.

5 When the eggplant is cool enough to handle, use a large spoon to
scrape the flesh from the skin. Discard the skins (although flecks
of char in the flesh are okay). Add the eggplant and 1½ teaspoons
of salt to the tomato mixture and use the large spoon to gently
mash everything, leaving some texture to the dip. Cook for about
5 minutes to allow the flavors to meld.

6 Add the lemon juice, taste for seasoning, then scoop the dip into
a serving bowl. Top with a drizzle of olive oil, the pistachios, and
additional parsley and cilantro. Serve with khobz or pita, for dipping.

Brown Bag Microwave Popcorn

⅓ cup **popcorn kernels**

Seasonings of choice

Corn was domesticated over 10,000 years ago in Mexico, but the first popcorn likely popped up in Peru around 4700 BCE. Fast-forward through a quick 6,000 years of history, and we find the microwave popcorn bag in 1981. It's safe to say that freshly popped popcorn is *the* staple snack for gathering around the TV, an accompaniment for everything from sports to movies. Translating that same concept to the brown-paper lunch sack loses none of the ease, plus it ups the game with endless combos of flavors. This recipe has it in the bag!

Add the corn kernels to a brown paper lunch bag. Fold the top of the bag twice to seal it tightly. Place the bag in the microwave and microwave on high for 2 to 3 minutes, until there are 2-second pauses between pops. Remove the bag and carefully open the top. Add any seasonings you like, fold the bag again, and shake to season the popped corn. Pour the popcorn into a bowl and serve.

SOME OF OUR FAVORITE TOPPINGS ARE:

- Melted butter
- Nutritional yeast
- Old Bay seasoning
- Furikake seasoning
- Tajin seasoning
- Chopped dried rosemary and Parmesan cheese
- Italian seasoning
- Ranch seasoning
- Hot sauce
- Caramel sauce
- Togarashi spice blend
- BBQ rub
- Za'atar spice blend

Fried Green Tomatoes with Zesty Buttermilk

Serves 4

FOR THE BUTTERMILK DRESSING

1 cup **mayonnaise**

½ cup **buttermilk**

1 teaspoon grated **lemon zest**

1 tablespoon **fresh lemon juice**

1 teaspoon **dried chives**

1 teaspoon **Italian seasoning**

FOR THE TOMATOES

2 pounds **green (unripe) tomatoes**, sliced into ¼-inch rounds

Kosher salt and **freshly ground black pepper**

1 cup **all-purpose flour**

1 teaspoon **garlic powder**

1 teaspoon **smoked paprika**

¼ teaspoon **cayenne pepper**

4 large **eggs**

2 tablespoons **whole milk**

2 cups **panko crumbs**

1 tablespoon **Italian seasoning**

2 quarts **vegetable oil**

Fried green tomatoes, considered a traditional Southern side dish, actually has almost no history in the South. Historians have traced recipes for fried green tomatoes to midwestern, northeastern, and Jewish-American cookbooks from the late 1800s, but mentions of the dish are all but nonexistent in that period's Southern cookbooks or in local newspapers. It wasn't until the 1991 movie *Fried Green Tomatoes*, in which some of the action takes place in a real café in Alabama, that the dish started gaining popularity. (Just like ratatouille, sometimes it takes a movie to make a dish a household name!) But when the green tomato slices are given a seasoned coating, fried, and then dipped in a zesty buttermilk dressing, they taste like they were born and raised in the South.

1 Make the buttermilk dressing: In a medium bowl, whisk together the mayonnaise, buttermilk, lemon zest and juice, chives, and Italian seasoning. Cover with plastic wrap and refrigerate.

2 Make the tomatoes: Season the tomato slices with salt and pepper on both sides.

3 In a shallow bowl, whisk together the flour, garlic powder, smoked paprika, and cayenne with a pinch of salt. In another shallow bowl, whisk together the eggs and milk with a pinch of salt. In a third shallow bowl, mix the panko and Italian seasoning with a pinch of salt.

4 In a Dutch oven or large heavy pot, heat the oil over medium-high heat. Use an instant-read thermometer to check periodically until the oil hits 350°F.

5 Working in batches, thoroughly coat the tomatoes in the flour mixture, then shake off the excess flour. Dip the slices in the egg mixture, coating both sides, and let the excess egg drip off. Then coat in the panko mixture, patting to adhere the crumbs. Working in batches, drop the tomatoes into the hot oil and fry until golden brown, about 2 minutes per side. Transfer to a plate lined with paper towels to drain.

6 Arrange the fried green tomatoes on a large serving plate and accompany with the dipping sauce.

Tropical Fruit Cocktail

½ small **papaya**, peeled (see Note), cut in half, seeds discarded, and flesh cut into ½-inch cubes

½ small **honeydew melon**, peeled (see Note), cut in half, seeds discarded, and flesh cut into ½-inch cubes

½ small **cantaloupe**, peeled (see Note), cut in half, seeds discarded, and flesh cut into ½-inch cubes

1 **mango**, peeled (see Note), seed removed, and flesh cut into ½-inch cubes

2 **kiwifruits**, peeled and cut into ½-inch cubes

Zest and juice of **1 lime**

2 tablespoons **honey**

Chili powder and toasted **coconut flakes**, for serving

Fruit salads are not only super refreshing but they're also super versatile. Many countries combine them with savory flavors, like the spicy Malaysian rojak with peanuts and shrimp paste, or the American Waldorf salad with apples, grapes, celery, walnuts, and mayonnaise. There are also sweet takes, like the Filipino buko salad or Mexican bionico, both of which use coconut and condensed milk. And sometimes we're doing both at once, like the Moroccan tradition of serving fruit salads alongside a variety of appetizers. This fruit salad, overflowing with ripe tropical fruits, is sweetened with honey, a touch of bitter lime zest, and a sprinkle of savory chili powder. It's just enough to feed—and please—a crowd.

Add the cubes of fruit to a large bowl. Whisk the lime zest and juice with the honey in a small bowl, then pour it over the fruit and toss to combine. Divide the fruit among eight serving cups. Sprinkle a few pinches of chili powder over the tops and finish with a pinch of coconut flakes before serving.

Helpful Hint

To peel a papaya: Gently run a vegetable peeler over the surface, applying enough pressure to peel but careful not to scrape into the fruit.

To peel a melon: Slice ½ inch from the top and bottom of the melon. Stand the melon up on one of the cut sides. Starting from the top and following the curve of the melon, slice the rind off in segments, rotating the melon as you go. Cut about ¼ inch deep, just enough to clear the green rind.

To peel a mango: Slice ¼ inch off the stem end. Stand the mango up on the cut side and slice down each side, as close to the seed as possible, to create 2 large segments. Cup one of the segments in your hand and use a tablespoon to scoop out the flesh. Cut any remaining mango flesh from the sides of the seed.

To peel a kiwi: Slice both ends off, then slide a spoon just under the peel and around the fruit to separate the peel from the flesh.

Pigs in a Blanket Pull-Apart Bread

Nonstick cooking spray

4 tablespoons (½ stick) **unsalted butter**, melted

1 teaspoon **dried oregano**

½ teaspoon **dry mustard**

½ teaspoon **garlic powder**

½ teaspoon **onion powder**

2 (8-ounce) tubes **crescent rolls**

6 slices **American cheese**

2 (12-ounce) packages **cocktail wieners**

Ketchup and **mustard**, for serving

A surprising number of countries in the world have a type of wrapped sausage. There's the German Würstchen im Schlafrock (sausage in a dressing gown), Israel's Moshe Ba'Teiva (Moses in the basket), Danish Pølsehorn (sausage horns), Mexican salchitaco (sausage taco), Chinese lop cheung bao or cheung jai bau (sausage bun), and most adorably, Scotland's kilted sausages. The American tradition of serving cocktail wieners wrapped in crescent rolls gets a real glow-up with this pull-apart bread, making a tasty treat that is oddly elegant and supremely delicious!

1 Preheat the oven to 350°F and set a rack in the center. Thoroughly coat a 10-inch Bundt pan with nonstick spray.

2 In a small bowl, whisk together the butter, oregano, dry mustard, garlic powder, and onion powder.

3 Unroll the crescent dough and brush the entire surface with the butter mixture. Separate the dough into 16 triangles, then cut each triangle lengthwise into 3 narrow triangles.

4 Cut each slice of American cheese into 8 pieces. Set a piece of cheese and a cocktail wiener on the widest edge of the buttered dough, then roll up to the point. Continue rolling and then arrange the finished wieners in the Bundt pan in alternating directions for a random pattern.

5 Bake for about 50 minutes, until the crescent dough is golden brown and cooked through. Set a baking pan over the Bundt pan, then invert and gently tap the pan to release the bread. Set a plate over the bread and flip again so the top is facing up. Allow the bread to cool for about 10 minutes, then serve with bowls of ketchup and mustard for dipping.

Just Desserts

PERFECT
each serves 4
PUDDING CUPS

Pudding is the world's great unifier. So many countries have a classic pudding dish, like French crème brûlée, Indian kheer, Italian panna cotta, endless riffs on muhallebi in the Middle East, and a wide variety of flans throughout Latin America. To add some pizazz to the treasured American pudding cup (has there ever been a more perfect vessel for pudding?) we took cues from sombi, a rich Senglese coconut and rice pudding; matcha purin, a Japanese masterpiece of umami and sweet; the spiced complexity of Mexican hot chocolate; and—why not?—the joy of an American classic, made with Funfetti sprinkles!

American Funfetti

2 tablespoons **cornstarch**

6 tablespoons **sugar**

¼ teaspoon **kosher salt**

2 cups **whole milk**

2 tablespoons **unsalted butter**, very cold

1 teaspoon **vanilla extract**

¼ cup **Funfetti sprinkles**

1 In a medium saucepan, whisk together the cornstarch, sugar, and salt. Add about ½ cup of the milk and whisk until smooth, then whisk in the remaining milk.

2 Set the saucepan over medium heat and cook, whisking continually, for about 10 minutes, until the pudding is bubbling and thick.

3 Remove the saucepan from the heat and whisk in the butter and vanilla. As soon as the butter is melted and blended in, transfer the pudding to an airtight container. Press plastic wrap onto the surface of the pudding, cover the container, and chill in the refrigerator for at least 2 hours or up to 24 hours. Fold in the sprinkles just before serving.

Mexican Hot Chocolate

2 tablespoons **cornstarch**

6 tablespoons **sugar**

2 tablespoons **unsweetened cocoa powder**

¼ teaspoon **kosher salt**

¼ teaspoon **ground cinnamon**

Pinch of **cayenne pepper**

2 cups **whole milk**

2 tablespoons **unsalted butter**, very cold

1 teaspoon **vanilla extract**

1 In a medium saucepan, whisk together the cornstarch, sugar, cocoa powder, salt, cinnamon, and cayenne. Add about ½ cup of the milk and whisk until smooth, then whisk in the remaining milk.

2 Set the saucepan over medium heat and cook, whisking continually, for about 10 minutes, until the pudding is bubbling and thick.

3 Remove the saucepan from the heat and whisk in the butter and vanilla. As soon as the butter is melted and blended in, transfer the pudding to an airtight container. Press plastic wrap onto the surface of the pudding, cover the container, and chill in the refrigerator for at least 2 hours or up to 24 hours before serving.

Senegalese Sombi

¼ cup cooked **white rice**

1 cup **full-fat coconut milk**

6 tablespoons **sugar**

¼ teaspoon **kosher salt**

2 tablespoons **cornstarch**

½ cup **coconut cream**

2 tablespoons **unsalted butter**, very cold

1 In a medium saucepan, whisk together the rice, coconut milk, sugar, and salt. Set over medium-high heat and cook, stirring, until the milk starts to simmer, then cover the saucepan, reduce the heat to low, and simmer for 20 minutes, until the rice is extra plump.

2 In a small bowl, whisk together the cornstarch and coconut cream until smooth. Whisk the cornstarch mixture into the rice mixture until well blended. Increase the heat to medium and continue whisking for about 10 minutes, until the pudding is bubbling and thick.

3 Remove the saucepan from the heat and whisk in the butter. As soon as the butter is melted and blended in, transfer it to an airtight container. Press plastic wrap onto the surface of the pudding, cover the container, and chill in the refrigerator for at least 2 hours or up to 24 hours before serving.

Japanese Matcha

2 tablespoons **cornstarch**

6 tablespoons **sugar**

¼ teaspoon **kosher salt**

2 cups **whole milk**

2 tablespoons **unsalted butter**, very cold

1 teaspoon **matcha powder**

1 In a medium saucepan, whisk together the cornstarch, sugar, and salt. Add about ½ cup of the milk and whisk until smooth, then whisk in the remaining milk.

2 Set the saucepan over medium heat and cook, whisking continually, for about 10 minutes, until the pudding is bubbling and thick.

3 Remove the saucepan from the heat and whisk in the butter and matcha. As soon as the butter is melted and blended in, transfer the pudding to an airtight container. Press plastic wrap onto the surface of the pudding, cover the container, and chill in the refrigerator for at least 2 hours or up to 24 hours before serving.

Kitchen Sink Pizookie

½ cup (1 stick) **unsalted butter**

½ cup **granulated sugar**

½ cup **dark brown sugar**

2 teaspoons **vanilla extract**

1 **large egg**

1 cup **all-purpose flour**

½ teaspoon **baking powder**

½ teaspoon **kosher salt**

½ cup **semisweet chocolate chips,** plus more for topping

½ cup **white chocolate chips,** plus more for topping

½ cup **lightly salted peanuts,** plus more for topping

½ cup **pretzel M&M's,** plus more for topping

Ice cream, for serving

The Pizookie—a pizza-sized cookie, for the uninitiated—is a dessert with a perfect balance of excess and perfection. This warm and gooey cookie (is there a better type of cookie?) that just happens to be the size of a skillet, is loaded with chocolate chips, nuts, and candy, then topped with a scoop of slowly melting ice cream. There's no other answer but to grab a spoon and dive in!

1 Preheat the oven to 350°F and set a rack in the center.

2 In a 10-inch cast-iron skillet, melt the butter over low heat. Allow the butter to slowly melt without bubbling.

3 Pour the melted butter into a large bowl, leaving a skim of melted butter in the skillet. Add the granulated sugar and brown sugar to the bowl and into the butter. Add the vanilla and egg and whisk until the egg is fully incorporated into the butter mixture. Add the flour, baking powder, and salt and use a rubber spatula to fold together, forming a cohesive dough. Add the ½ cup each chocolate chips, white chips, peanuts, and M&M's, and continue folding until the ingredients are well blended.

4 Transfer the cookie dough to the skillet, using the spatula to smooth it into an even layer. Bake for 25 to 30 minutes, until the center is just barely set and still a little gooey.

5 Remove the skillet from the oven and immediately sprinkle the top of the Pizookie with additional chocolate chips, white chocolate chips, peanuts, and M&M's. Add a large scoop of ice cream (or two!) to the center of the Pizookie and serve immediately, with spoons.

Berry-Layered Jell-O Mold

Nonstick cooking spray

1 (3-ounce) box **strawberry Jell-O** mix

¾ cup hulled and quartered **fresh strawberries**

¾ cup **fresh raspberries**

1 (3-ounce) box **orange Jell-O** mix

¾ cup drained **canned mandarin orange segments**

¾ cup drained **canned pineapple chunks**

1 (3-ounce) box **lemon Jell-O** mix

1 (14-ounce) can **sweetened condensed milk**

Helpful Hint
Letting each layer cool completely may seem time-consuming, but it's the only way to achieve a perfectly layered confection.

Jell-O was invented in 1897 in Le Roy, New York. (You already know there's a Jell-O Museum.) Originally meant to be a dessert, Jell-O hit an interesting peak in the 1950s, serving as a mold for savory salads, meats, and even pasta. Brace yourself: it gets worse. In response to all these savory Jell-O uses, the brand introduced flavors like celery, mixed vegetable, and seasoned tomato. In more sensible times, like now, we honor Jell-O's place as a satisfying dessert—and *only* as a dessert. This layered mold, loaded with bright fruits and jiggling attractively, is absolutely the most beautiful that Jell-O has ever looked.

1 Thoroughly spray a 10-inch Bundt pan with nonstick spray.

2 In a medium bowl, make the strawberry Jell-O according to the package directions. Allow it to come to room temperature, about 30 minutes. Add the strawberries and raspberries to the bowl, then pour the mixture into the Bundt pan. Cover with plastic wrap and refrigerate for at least 4 hours, until fully set.

3 In a medium bowl, make the orange Jell-O according to the package directions. Allow it to come to room temperature, about 30 minutes. Add the mandarin oranges and pineapple to the bowl, then pour the mixture over the strawberry mixture in the Bundt pan. Cover the pan again and refrigerate for at least another 4 hours, until fully set.

4 In a medium bowl, make the lemon Jell-O according to the package directions. Allow it to come to room temperature, about 30 minutes. Stir in the condensed milk, then pour the mixture over the orange mixture in the Bundt pan. Cover the pan again and refrigerate for at least another 4 hours, until fully set.

5 Remove the Bundt pan from the refrigerator. Use a finger to make sure the Jell-O easily pulls away from the sides and center tube of the pan. Place a large serving plate over the pan and invert the pan to allow the Jell-O mold to drop down. Serve immediately.

Cherry Dr Pepper Cake

FOR THE LAYER CAKES

Nonstick cooking spray

3 large eggs

⅓ cup **vegetable oil**

1 (15.25-ounce) box **red velvet chocolate cake mix**

1 (12-ounce) can **Dr Pepper**

FOR THE FROSTING

2 (8-ounce) packages **cream cheese**, room temperature

1 cup (2 sticks) **unsalted butter**, at room temperature

2 cups **powdered sugar**

1 (21-ounce) can **cherry pie filling** or **cherry preserves**

8 **cherry gummy candies**

Helpful Hint
Why turn the top layer upside down? It's the easiest way to guarantee a perfectly flat top!

Adding soda to a cake batter is a distinctly Southern tradition—no surprise since most soda companies are headquartered in the South. But cakes like 7-UP and Coca-Cola have spread far beyond the region to become staples of American home cooking. We decided to up the game with a Dr Pepper cake that is all cherry, all the time. The red velvet cake batter is enhanced with the subtle cherry notes in the soda, then it gets smothered in cherry frosting, loaded with cherry filling, and even topped with cherry gummies. Impressive, delicious, and easy to make, it's a guaranteed hit!

1 Make the layer cakes: Preheat the oven to 350°F and set a rack in the center. Spray two 8-inch round cake pans with nonstick spray.

2 In a large bowl, whisk together the eggs and oil. Add the cake mix and Dr Pepper, and whisk to combine. Divide the batter between the two pans and bake for 20 to 25 minutes, until a toothpick inserted in the center of the layers comes out clean. Let cool completely in the pans, about 2 hours.

3 Make the frosting: In a medium bowl, and using an electric hand mixer starting on low speed and working up to high, whip the cream cheese and butter until light and fluffy, about 3 minutes. Add the powdered sugar and ½ cup of the cherry pie filling. Whip again until fully blended and the cherries are in small pieces, about 2 minutes.

4 Place a small dab of frosting in the center of a cake stand to hold the cake in place. Remove one cooled layer from its pan and center it on the frosting. Use about 1 cup of frosting to spread a smooth, even layer across the cake. Spoon the remaining cherry pie filling over the frosting and smooth into an even layer.

5 Remove the remaining cake from its pan and flip upside down and lay it on top of the frosting. Use about ½ cup of the frosting to create a thin crumb coat around the outside edge of the cake. Use another ½ cup of the frosting to apply a thin layer to the top of the cake. Transfer the cake to the refrigerator and chill for 30 minutes to set the first layer.

6 Use the remaining frosting to generously frost the outside and top of the cake, swooping and swirling it in attractive patterns. Lay the cherry gummies around the perimeter of the cake top, then slice and serve.

A

B

C

D

E

Key Lime Cheesecake Pops

FOR THE CRUST

Nonstick cooking spray

9 whole **graham crackers**

¼ cup **sweetened shredded coconut**

6 tablespoons (¾ stick) **unsalted butter**, melted

¼ teaspoon **kosher salt**

FOR THE FILLING

1½ (8-ounce) packages **cream cheese**, softened

2 cups **powdered sugar**

2 tablespoons **fresh lime juice**

1 tablespoon grated **lime zest**, plus more for serving

1 teaspoon **vanilla extract**

½ teaspoon **kosher salt**

½ cup **heavy cream**

Whipped cream, for serving

Key lime pie, an undisputed American classic, originated in Key West, Florida. But the fruit that became the Key lime itself took a long journey from its home in Southeast Asia, moved via the spice trade through the Middle East, North Africa, Sicily, and Andalusia, before it was brought by Spanish explorers to the Caribbean, Mexico, and—finally!—the Florida Keys. In place of a traditional pie, we opted here for a frozen treat that's as easy to make as it is to eat, thanks to a handy popsicle stick. In 1965, a state representative in Florida introduced legislation that would fine anyone making Key lime pie without using Key limes; lucky for us, that bill failed. So, grab whatever limes you have on hand and get going!

1 Make the crust: Grease a 9-inch round tart pan with nonstick spray.

2 Add the graham crackers to a large ziptop plastic bag. Seal and use a rolling pin to crush into fine crumbs.

3 In a medium bowl, combine the graham cracker crumbs, the coconut, butter, and salt. Stir to form a mixture that resembles wet sand. Pour the mixture into the prepared pan, then press with your fingers to spread in an even layer across the bottom and up the sides.

4 Make the filling: Place the cream cheese in a large bowl. Use an electric hand mixer at medium speed to beat until smooth. Add the powdered sugar, lime juice and 1 tablespoon lime zest, the vanilla, salt, and cream. Continue to whip until stiff peaks form, 2 to 3 minutes.

5 Pour the filling into the crust, smoothing the top with a rubber spatula. Place the pan in the freezer for 30 minutes. Remove the pan from the freezer and set the base of the pan atop a large jar. Carefully slide the side of the tart pan down to unmold the tart, then take the tart on its base off the jar and set on a work surface.

6 Insert 8 popsicle sticks through the sides of the crust, into the center of the tart, spacing them evenly around the circumference. Decorate the top of the tart with some whipped cream and sprinkle on more lime zest.

7 Freeze the tart for 4 hours, until the filling is fully set. When ready to serve, cut the tart into 8 slices, one popsicle stick per serving.

Fried Mini Oreo Bites

1 (17-ounce) tube **flaky biscuit dough**

1 (3.5-ounce) package **mini Oreo cookies**

2 quarts **vegetable oil**

¾ cup **powdered sugar**

1 tablespoon **whole milk**

Charlie Boghosian, born in Syria to Armenian parents, emigrated to America when he was 11. At 14 years old, he started working as a food vendor at country fairs in Southern California. Why are we talking about him? Well, in 2004 he changed life as we know it by introducing the fried Oreo at the L.A. County Fair. Already one of the most delicious treats in the world, this recipe makes it one of the easiest, too. The mini Oreos get wrapped in biscuit dough and are quickly fried for a fast dessert whenever the craving strikes!

1 Separate the biscuits and cut each round into quarters. Flatten 1 quarter with your fingers, then place a mini Oreo in the center. Pinch the biscuit dough around it, to seal as tightly as possible. Repeat with the remaining dough rounds to make 24 pieces.

2 Place the remaining Oreos in a large ziptop plastic bag and use a rolling pin to crush to fine crumbs.

3 In a Dutch oven or large heavy pot, heat the oil over medium-high heat. Use an instant-read thermometer to check periodically until the oil hits 350°F.

4 Working in batches, drop the Oreo bites into the hot oil, turning occasionally, until golden brown, about 2 minutes. Remove to a plate lined with paper towels to drain.

5 In a small bowl, stir together the powdered sugar and milk to form a smooth glaze. One by one, dip the Oreo bites in the glaze, then place on a serving plate. Sprinkle the crushed Oreo cookies over the tops while the glaze is still wet and serve immediately.

Stuffed Peanut Butter Bars

9 **white** or **milk chocolate peanut butter cups**

18 whole **graham crackers**

1 cup (2 sticks) **unsalted butter**

1¼ cups **creamy peanut butter**

2 cups **powdered sugar**

1 (12-ounce) bag **semisweet chocolate chips**

For fans of chocolate and peanut butter, there's no such thing as too much chocolate or peanut butter. Those classic no-bake peanut butter bars—a staple of grandma's house and bake sales—get pushed one step further with the addition of peanut butter cups inside. The cups not only provide a perfect base for the bar, they also offer a peanutty bonus with each bite. Win-win!

Helpful Hint

Binder clips keep the parchment in place for an easy, breezy removal process. But be sure to use the all-metal clips; plastic in the oven is never a good idea.

1 Line an 8-inch square baking pan with two 10 by 8-inch pieces of parchment paper, leaving a 2-inch overhang on two sides. Use binder clips to fasten the parchment firmly in place.

2 Evenly space the peanut butter cups in the pan.

3 In a food processor or blender, place the graham crackers and pulse about 10 times to create fine crumbs. (Alternatively, place the graham crackers in a ziptop plastic bag and use a rolling pin to create fine crumbs.) You should have almost 2 cups of crumbs.

4 Place the butter in a medium microwave-safe bowl and microwave on high for 1 to 2 minutes, until the butter is almost completely melted. Whisk in 1 cup of the peanut butter and the powdered sugar to create a smooth mixture. Use a rubber spatula to fold in the graham cracker crumbs. Use clean hands to scoop up and press the mixture into the pan, covering the peanut butter cups with an even layer of the crumb mixture.

5 Place the chocolate chips and the remaining ¼ cup peanut butter in the bowl and microwave on high for about 2 minutes, stopping to stir every 30 seconds, until the chips are almost completely melted. Stir into a smooth, cohesive mixture, then pour into the pan. Run a rubber spatula back and forth across the chocolate to smooth it into an even layer, adding some swooping texture.

6 Cover the pan with plastic wrap, being careful not to let it touch the chocolate layer. Let sit in a cool, dry place for at least 1 hour, until the chocolate has slightly firmed.

7 Using the overhanging parchment, lift the cake out of the pan and set it on a cutting board. Slice into 9 large squares, then slice each square in half to reveal the peanut butter cup within. Serve immediately or transfer to an airtight container and refrigerate. Bring to room temperature before serving.

Spumoni Sundae Brownies

Nonstick cooking spray

1 (18.3-ounce) box **fudge brownie mix**, plus additional ingredients according to box instructions

1 (8-ounce) package **cream cheese**, softened

1 cup **powdered sugar**

1 cup **cherry pie filling**

2 (8-ounce) containers **frozen whipped topping**, thawed

2 (3.4-ounce) boxes **pistachio pudding mix**

2 cups **whole milk**, very cold

½ cup chopped **pistachios**

Chocolate sprinkles, whipped cream, and **maraschino cherries**, for serving

Helpful Hint

While slicing the brownies, keep a dish towel nearby to wipe your knife after each cut for clean and neat servings.

Spumoni came to America in the 1870s with Italian immigrants from Naples. Traditionally a stack of three layers of gelato (usually vanilla or chocolate, cherry, and pistachio), which is served sliced, not scooped, spumoni is a staple of Little Italy restaurants across the country. For an easy home-style dessert, we employ a box of brownies, a can of cherry pie filling, and a package of pistachio pudding to achieve the total comfort flavors with none of the melting mess. Bravo!

1 Preheat the oven to 350°F and set a rack in the center. Generously coat a 9 by 13-inch baking pan with nonstick spray.

2 Prepare the brownie mix, following the directions for cake-like brownies. Pour the batter into the prepared baking pan and bake until a toothpick inserted into the center comes out clean. Let cool completely, about 1 hour.

3 In a large bowl, using a hand electric mixer, combine the cream cheese, powdered sugar, and cherry pie filling on low speed until smooth, about 2 minutes. Gently fold in one container of the whipped topping. Scrape and smooth the cherry mixture over the brownies. Cover with plastic wrap and chill for 2 hours.

4 In a medium bowl, whisk together the pudding mix and milk for about 2 minutes, until slightly thickened. Cover with plastic wrap and let rest for about 10 minutes, until fully set. Gently fold in the pistachios and remaining container of whipped topping. Scrape and smooth the pistachio mixture over the cherry layer. Cover with plastic wrap and chill for 4 hours or up to 24 hours.

5 Sprinkle the layered brownie with chocolate sprinkles, then dot with whipped cream and cherries. Slice and serve immediately.

Egyptian Pumpkin Pie

Nonstick cooking spray

5 pounds peeled and chopped
fresh butternut squash

2 cups **sugar**

1 cup **slivered almonds**

½ cup **raisins**

½ cup **unsweetened shredded
coconut**

1 teaspoon **ground cardamom**

1 teaspoon **ground cinnamon**

2 tablespoons **samna** or **ghee**
(clarified butter)

2 tablespoons **all-purpose flour**

2 cups **whole milk**

1 teaspoon **vanilla extract**

Honey, for serving

For anyone who has ever stressed about making a great pie crust—that's all of us, right?—we have the perfect solution: pie without a crust! Kar' assaly, "pumpkin pie" in Arabic, has all the warm spices and total comfort we expect when we hear those magic words. The winter squash we know and love as pumpkin is native to North America, so in other parts of the world the word "pumpkin" is often more generally applied— in this case, to butternut squash. A mix of almonds, raisins, and coconut adds amazing texture, while cardamom and cinnamon contribute the perfect spice, and a milky topping bubbles and browns as the pie bakes. It might be time to welcome a new tradition into your home!

1 Preheat the oven to 400°F and set a rack in the center. Generously coat a 9 by 13-inch baking pan with nonstick spray.

2 In a Dutch oven or large heavy pot, combine the squash and sugar. Set the pot over medium heat and carefully stir until the squash has started to release some liquid. Cover the pot and increase the heat to medium-high. Simmer, stirring occasionally with a wooden spoon, until the squash is soft and covered with liquid, about 15 minutes.

3 In a medium bowl, combine the almonds, raisins, and coconut.

4 Use a ladle to remove ½ cup of the liquid from the squash and set aside. Continue simmering, uncovered, stirring often until the rest of the liquid is almost completely evaporated, about 15 minutes. Add the cardamom and cinnamon and use a wooden spoon to roughly mash the squash.

5 Spread half the squash mixture in the prepared baking pan. Sprinkle half the almond mixture over the squash, then add the remaining squash mixture and sprinkle on the remaining almond mixture.

6 In the same pot, melt the samna over medium heat. Add the flour and whisk until light golden brown, about 2 minutes. Slowly whisk in the milk and continue whisking until the mixture is very thick, about 3 minutes. Remove from the heat and whisk in the vanilla and reserved squash liquid.

7 Pour the milk mixture onto the squash layers in the baking pan. Bake for 30 to 35 minutes, until dark brown on the edges and golden in the center. Cool for 15 minutes before scooping and serving with a drizzle of honey.

Texas Sheet Cake with Candied Pecans

Serves 16

FOR THE CAKE

Nonstick cooking spray

¼ cup unsweetened **cocoa powder**

1 cup (2 sticks) **unsalted butter**

2 cups **all-purpose flour**

1½ cups **granulated sugar**

½ cup **dark brown sugar**

1 tablespoon **instant coffee**

1 teaspoon **baking soda**

½ teaspoon **kosher salt**

½ cup **buttermilk**

2 large eggs

FOR THE PECANS

2 cups **pecans**, roughly chopped

¼ cup **dark brown sugar**

FOR THE FROSTING

1½ cups (3 sticks) **unsalted butter**, at room temperature

5 cups **powdered sugar**

1 cup unsweetened **cocoa powder**

¼ cup **buttermilk**, plus more as needed

2 teaspoons **vanilla extract**

Flaky sea salt, for serving

A classic of recipe cards, potlucks, even funerals, this sheet cake is as synonymous with Texas as the pecans on top. A recipe for German's Chocolate Cake was first published in a Dallas newspaper in 1957, but contrary to popular belief, the cake wasn't from Germany. It was named for Sam German, a chocolatier in Massachusetts who formulated a sweet baking chocolate. Today it goes by any combo of names—Texas Sheet Cake, Funeral Cake, or German Chocolate—but we just call it one thing: delicious!

1 Make the cake: Preheat the oven to 350°F and set a rack in the center. Coat an 18 by 13-inch rimmed baking sheet with nonstick spray.

2 In a medium saucepan, bring 1 cup of water to a boil over high heat. Add the cocoa powder and whisk to combine. Add the butter and remove from the heat, allowing the butter to slowly melt.

3 In a large bowl, whisk together the flour, granulated sugar, brown sugar, coffee, baking soda, and salt. When the butter has melted, add the cocoa mixture to the flour mixture and whisk to incorporate. Add the buttermilk and eggs and whisk again to form a smooth batter.

4 Pour the batter into the prepared baking sheet and bake for about 20 minutes, until a toothpick inserted in the center comes out clean. Cool completely on the baking sheet. Maintain the oven temperature at 350°F.

5 Make the pecans: Line a rimmed baking sheet with parchment paper. In a medium bowl, toss together the pecans, brown sugar, and 1 tablespoon of water. Spread the pecans on the prepared baking sheet and bake for about 15 minutes, stirring halfway, until the pecans are toasted and the coating is caramelized.

6 Make the frosting: Add the butter to a large bowl and use a hand mixer to beat on medium speed until light and fluffy, about 2 minutes. Add the powdered sugar, cocoa powder, buttermilk, and vanilla. Start beating on low speed and increase to high speed, then beat for about 1 minute until the frosting is smooth and airy. If the frosting is too thick, add another tablespoon of buttermilk to thin it slightly.

7 Spread the frosting across the top of the cooled cake and then sprinkle with the candied pecans. Chill the cake for up to 24 hours or serve immediately with a sprinkle of flaky sea salt over the top.

Apple Pie a la Mode Sundae

FOR THE CINNAMON SAUCE

½ cup **dark brown sugar**

1 tablespoon **cornstarch**

2 tablespoons **unsalted butter**

1 teaspoon **ground cinnamon**

½ teaspoon **vanilla extract**

½ teaspoon **kosher salt**

FOR THE BROWNED BUTTER APPLES

2 tablespoons **unsalted butter**

1 medium **Granny Smith apple,** peeled, cored, and diced in ½-inch pieces

⅛ teaspoon **ground nutmeg**

⅛ teaspoon **ground cloves**

FOR THE SUNDAE

Vanilla ice cream

4 individual **graham crackers** (one 4-piece rectangle)

Whipped cream and **ground nutmeg,** for serving

Apple pie is a symbol of the United States, the star of our comfort food, as American as . . . apple pie. Well, we hate to say it, but it's all a lie (except the comfort food part). Apple pies were popular in England and the Netherlands as far back as the Middle Ages, but when apples were brought to the American colonies, they were mostly used to make cider. It wasn't until the later 1700s, as the colonies were becoming the United States, that apple pie started to gain popularity. So, maybe that symbolism holds up after all! The favorite American style for serving pie, a la mode, is taken to the extreme here with a sundae that is more like a scoop of "pie" on your ice cream. But with all the flavors you already know and love, it's the perfect excuse for a bite of comfort all the time.

1 Make the cinnamon sauce: In a small saucepan, whisk together the brown sugar and cornstarch. Add ½ cup of water and whisk until smooth. Add another ½ cup water and bring to a simmer over medium-low heat. Continue whisking constantly until the sauce is like a thin caramel, about 2 minutes. Remove from the heat and whisk in the butter until melted. Whisk in the cinnamon, vanilla, and salt and pour the mixture into a medium bowl.

2 Make the browned butter apples: In a medium skillet, melt the butter over medium heat. Continue cooking the butter, swirling the pan as it foams, until the butter begins to brown, about 2 minutes. Remove from the heat and stir for about 30 seconds, until deeply brown and fragrant.

3 Add the apples along with ¼ cup water and return the skillet to medium heat. Simmer, stirring occasionally, until the apples are tender, about 5 minutes. Remove from the heat and stir in the nutmeg and cloves.

4 Prepare the sundaes: Scoop the ice cream into four serving bowls. Divide the apples among the bowls and crumble 1 graham cracker over each sundae. Top with whipped cream, a sprinkle of nutmeg, and a drizzle of the cinnamon sauce. Serve immediately.

Eid Cookies

FOR THE COOKIES

3 cups **all-purpose flour**

3 tablespoons **sesame seeds, toasted**

1 tablespoon **granulated sugar**

1 teaspoon **instant yeast**

½ teaspoon **ground cinnamon**

¼ teaspoon **kosher salt**

1 cup **ghee** (clarified butter), room temperature

⅓ cup **warm water**

Powdered sugar, **for dusting**

FOR THE FILLING

1 tablespoon **ghee** (clarified butter)

1 tablespoon **all-purpose flour**

1 tablespoon **sesame seeds, toasted**

¼ cup **honey**

½ cup **pistachios**, finely chopped

Eid cookies, also known as ka'ak al-eid, have their origins in ancient Egypt. The cookies became associated with Islam during the Tulunid dynasty and became synonymous with Eid al-Fitr, the feast marking the end of Ramadan, during the Ikhshidid dynasty. The cookies were often imprinted with geometric designs, sayings like kol wishukr ("eat and say thank you"), and sometimes stuffed with coins. Today ka'ak are stuffed with a sweet filling, like dates, lokum (Turkish delight), or the honey-nut mixture in our recipe. A quick dusting of powdered sugar and they're ready for a celebration of food and family!

1 Make the cookies: In a large bowl, whisk together the flour, sesame seeds, granulated sugar, yeast, cinnamon, and salt. Add the ghee and ⅓ cup of warm water, and use an electric hand mixer on medium speed to beat into a soft, pliable dough, about 2 minutes. Cover the bowl with plastic wrap and let the dough rest for 1 hour.

2 Meanwhile, make the filling: In a small saucepan, melt the ghee over medium heat. Add the flour and whisk until golden brown and fragrant, about 2 minutes. Reduce the heat to low and add the sesame seeds and honey. Use a wooden spoon to stir until the mixture forms a thick paste, about 5 minutes. Remove from the heat and stir in the pistachios. Let cool for at least 15 minutes or up to 1 hour.

3 Preheat the oven to 375°F and set a rack in the center. Line a rimmed baking sheet with parchment paper.

4 Scoop up 1 rounded teaspoon of the filling at a time and roll it into a ball, making 20 pistachio balls. Then scoop up about 2 tablespoons of dough and roll it into a larger ball, making 20 dough balls. Press a pistachio ball into the center of each dough ball, then pinch the seams and roll into a smooth ball.

5 Arrange the balls on the prepared baking sheet. Lightly press the balls with the tines of a fork to make a crosshatch pattern or use a ma'amoul mold. Bake for 18 to 20 minutes, until the bottoms are golden brown. Transfer the cookies to a wire rack to cool completely, about 1 hour. Dust the cookies with powdered sugar just before serving.

Chocolate Halva Truffles

1 cup **powdered sugar**

½ cup **rice** or **coconut flour**, plus more as needed

½ teaspoon **kosher salt**

½ cup **tahini**, plus more as needed

6 ounces **70% dark chocolate**, chopped

1 tablespoon **refined coconut oil**

Finely chopped **pistachios**, toasted **sesame seeds**, **shredded coconut, flaky sea salt**, for topping

Helpful Hint

Setting a bowl over boiling water is an easy way to ensure the chocolate slowly melts into a silky pool. But it's important that the bowl isn't making contact with the water or it could overheat and scorch the chocolate.

Halva, from an Arabic root word meaning "sweet," originated in Persia as a mash of dates and milk. Over the centuries it has evolved into a popular treat throughout Asia, Europe, and Africa, with tons of variations. In the countries surrounding the Mediterranean, halva is commonly made with tahini and sugar, flavored with vanilla, pistachios, or chocolate, and packed into rectangular shapes ready to be sliced. This recipe cheats a little to make a very pliable halva, ready to be rolled into balls, dipped in chocolate, and topped with a variety of crunchy toppings. It's a perfect one-bite treat!

1 In a medium bowl, whisk together the powdered sugar, rice flour, and salt. Add the tahini and use clean hands to massage it into a thick paste. It might crumble at first, but keep working it until it comes together. Let rest for 5 minutes to hydrate until it can hold a firm ball shape. If it's still too crumbly to hold a ball shape, mix in 1 tablespoon of tahini and let it rest again. If it's too loose to hold a ball shape, mix in a tablespoon of rice flour and let it rest again.

2 Line a rimmed baking sheet with parchment paper. Scoop up a tablespoon of the mixture and roll it into a ball, then continue to make balls, lining them up on the prepared baking sheet. Let chill briefly in the refrigerator while making the chocolate.

3 Fill a medium saucepan with 2 inches of water and bring to a boil over high heat. Set a medium bowl on top of the saucepan, making sure the bottom of the bowl isn't touching the water. Add the chocolate and coconut oil. Use a rubber spatula to stir constantly as the chocolate melts. When the chocolate is almost completely melted, remove the bowl from the heat.

4 Drop a tahini ball into the warm chocolate and use a fork to roll it around, coating it completely. Lift out with the fork and let the excess chocolate drip off before setting the tahini ball pack on the baking sheet. Before the chocolate dries, sprinkle the ball with your choice of topping. Continue dipping the remaining tahini balls in the chocolate, setting the chocolate back over boiling water to reheat as needed.

5 Return the truffles to the refrigerator for 15 minutes to fully set the chocolate. Serve immediately, or transfer to an airtight container and refrigerate for up to 24 hours.

Cheers!

RETRO SODA
each serves 1
FOUNTAIN DRINKS

The classic American soda fountain hit its peak in the 1940s and 50s, with soda jerks serving ice cream sodas, phosphates, milkshakes, and light meals while throwing around jargon like "twist it, choke it, make it cackle" (that's a chocolate malted milkshake with a raw egg). While milkshakes sometimes had eggs and cream, the egg cream was oddly without either. And creative combos, like the forever-classic root beer float and lime rickey, are thanks to the genius minds behind the bar. So, go heavy on the hail, shake one, and add a snowball!

Root Beer Float

1 (12-ounce) can **root beer**, very cold

2 scoops **vanilla ice cream**

Whipped cream and **maraschino cherry**,
for serving

1 Fill a chilled pint glass one-third full with root beer. Add the ice cream. Tilt the glass and pour more root beer down the side of the glass. (This will give you more root beer and less foam.)

2 Top with whipped cream and a cherry before serving.

Malted Milkshake

2 tablespoons **whole milk**, very cold

2 tablespoons **vanilla** or **chocolate syrup**

2 tablespoons **malted milk powder**

2 scoops **vanilla** or **chocolate ice cream**

Whipped cream and **chocolate sprinkles**,
for serving

1 Add the milk, syrup, malted milk powder, and ice cream (in that order) to a blender. Blend on high speed until all the ingredients are combined into a thick shake.

2 Pour into a chilled milkshake glass and top with whipped cream and sprinkles before serving.

Helpful Hint

While all the ingredients should be super cold, the ice cream scoop should be hot. Fill a glass with hot tap water and soak your scoop for a few seconds. Scooping the ice cream will then be smooth and easy.

Classic Egg Cream

¼ cup **chocolate syrup**, preferably Fox's U-Bet
½ cup **whole milk**, very cold
Club soda or **seltzer water**, very cold

1 Pour the syrup into a chilled pint glass. Use a bar spoon to stir in the milk until well blended with the syrup.

2 Slowly pour the club soda straight into the glass until a thick foam comes up to the edge of the glass. Be careful not to spill over. Use the bar spoon to quickly stir just once (no more!) and mix everything. Serve immediately.

Lime Rickey

¼ cup **fresh lime juice** (from about 2 limes)
2 tablespoons **sugar**
1 teaspoon **maraschino syrup** plus **1 maraschino cherry**, for serving
Ice cubes
Club soda or **seltzer water**, very cold

1 Add the lime juice, sugar, and syrup to a chilled Collins glass. Use a bar spoon to stir until the sugar is dissolved.

2 Add ice to fill the glass, then top off with club soda. Garnish with a cherry before serving.

Helpful Hint

Don't have a bar spoon? Don't stress it! Just grab a chopstick and get stirring.

Fruit Punch Pouches

1 cup chopped **fresh watermelon**

4 **fresh mandarin oranges**, peeled and sectioned

½ cup chopped **fresh pineapple**

½ cup **coconut water**

2 ounces (4 tablespoons) **spiced rum** (optional)

Punch originated in India as a drink made with alcohol, citrus juice, water, sugar, and spices (the word punch may come from pāñć, the Hindi word for "five," because of the five ingredients). In America, fruit punch is most often found in juice boxes or pouches, without alcohol and without, well, any fruit. Here is an extra-fruity pouch of punch that's every bit as refreshing. And while some may say that adding a splash of alcohol is too wild, we say it's just respecting tradition!

Add the watermelon, mandarin oranges, pineapple, coconut water, and spiced rum (if using) to a blender. Blend on high speed for about 2 minutes, until completely smooth. Divide among the drink pouches and serve immediately or refrigerate for up to 24 hours.

Sweet Peach Iced Tea

Serves 8

4 bags **black tea**

1 cup **sugar**

2 **fresh peaches**, cut in half, pitted, and sliced, plus more for serving

1 (1-inch) piece **fresh ginger**, cut in half and sliced

10 **fresh mint leaves**, plus more for serving

Ice cubes, for serving

Helpful Hint

The longer tea steeps, the more tannins it releases, giving it a dry and sometimes bitter taste. Limit the steeping to 5 minutes for a perfectly balanced drink.

Tea originated as a medicinal drink in northeastern India and southwestern China, and later spread throughout East Asia as a mostly recreational drink. Portuguese traders brought tea to Europe, British colonizers started mass tea plantations in India, and after a brief protest in Boston Harbor, Americans sort of came around to drinking tea. In the 1860s and 70s, iced tea started to become the dominant tea in the United States, and sweet tea became the default version in the South. This little sweetie, flavored with peaches, a zing of ginger, and a hint of mint, is the ultimate porch drink no matter where you are!

1 In a large saucepan, bring 8 cups of water to a boil over high heat. Remove from the heat and when the water stops boiling, add the tea bags. Cover and steep for 5 minutes. Remove the tea bags; cover again and let cool completely, about 1 hour.

2 In a medium saucepan, bring 1 cup of water plus the sugar and the 2 peaches to a boil over high heat. Remove from the heat and add the ginger and the 10 mint leaves. Cover and let cool completely, about 1 hour.

3 Set a fine-mesh strainer over the tea and pour in the peach syrup. Discard the peaches, ginger, and mint. Pour the sweetened tea into a large pitcher. Serve in glasses filled with ice and garnish with mint and peach slices.

Frozen Pink Lemonade

½ cup **fresh lemon juice** (from 2 large lemons)

½ cup **sugar**

½ cup **unsweetened cranberry juice**

1 (7.5-ounce) can **lemon-lime soda** or ½ cup **Fireball Cinnamon Whisky**

Lemon wheels, for serving

Back in the day—that is, the 1200s BCE in Egypt—a drink made with lemons, dates, and honey was gaining popularity. Fast-forward a few centuries to 1800s America, where a 15-year-old Henry E. "Sanchez" Allot ran away to join the circus. He was working the lemonade stand and he accidentally dropped red cinnamon candies into the vat, giving birth to pink lemonade! (There's another origin story where Pete Conklin, another circus employee, used a tub of water, in which a horse rider had just washed her red tights, to make a batch of pink lemonade. But we're sticking to the not-gross story.) This frozen lemonade uses a more sensible cranberry juice for a perfectly pink color. Make it with soda for an extra-sweet kick or, in a tip of the hat to Henry, a little cinnamon whisky for a spicy kick!

1 In a large liquid measuring cup or a container with a spout, whisk together the lemon juice, sugar, cranberry juice, and 1¼ cups of water. Carefully pour the mixture into an ice cube tray and freeze for at least 8 hours or up to 24 hours.

2 Add the frozen lemonade to a blender along with the lemon-lime soda. Blend on high speed until smooth and icy, about 2 minutes. Divide among eight glasses and serve with the lemon wheels.

Sparkling Spa Water

Serves 8

1 **fresh grapefruit**, cut in half, then cut into quarters

1 **fresh blood orange**, thinly sliced

6 **fresh mandarin oranges**, peeled and segments separated

1 **fresh cucumber**, thinly sliced

1 large sprig **fresh mint**, stemmed

Club soda or **seltzer water**, for serving

The word "spa" comes from the town of Spa, Belgium, known for its natural mineral springs, where centuries of Europeans would flock to drink the healing waters. (Let's just quickly acknowledge that medicine has come a long way.) But this definitely answers the question of why today's day spas always have the best water. This pitcher of spa water, loaded with vitamin C–rich fruits, cooling cucumbers, and soothing mint, is not only more delicious than those canned fruit seltzers but it's also much cooler to offer your friends a glass of *spa water*.

1 In a large pitcher, layer the pieces of grapefruit, orange, mandarin oranges, and cucumber, and the mint leaves in alternating patterns. Fill with cold filtered water. Cover with plastic wrap and chill for at least 1 hour or up to 24 hours.

2 To serve, use a wooden spoon to scoop some of the fruit into a glass, fill the glass halfway, then top off with the club soda. Serve.

Note: You can top off the pitcher with more filtered water up to two more times, covering and chilling the pitcher in between servings.

Helpful Hint

What's the difference between club soda and seltzer? They're both filtered water that's been pumped with carbonation, but club soda is enhanced with minerals like potassium bicarbonate and potassium sulfate, which give it some saltiness and enhance the flavor when added to drinks.

Puerto Rican Coquito

1 (12-ounce) can **evaporated milk**

1 (14-ounce) can **sweetened condensed milk**

1 (15-ounce) can **cream of coconut**

1 (13.5-ounce) can **full-fat coconut milk**

1 cup **white rum** (optional)

1 teaspoon **vanilla extract**

½ teaspoon **ground cinnamon, plus more as needed**

¼ teaspoon **ground nutmeg**

Cinnamon sticks, for serving

Coquito (little coconut) is a traditional Puerto Rican holiday drink, like eggnog but ten times better. Sweet, coconutty, boozy, and perfectly spiced, coquito goes down maybe a little too easy (make a double batch!). It can be served same-day, but it reaches peak flavor if refrigerated for up to two weeks ahead. Just remember to give the bottle a good shake every day (and sneak a sip).

1 In a large bowl, whisk together the evaporated milk, condensed milk, cream of coconut, coconut milk, rum (if using), vanilla, ½ teaspoon cinnamon, and the nutmeg. Divide the mixture among large bottles or jars, close tightly, and refrigerate for at least 2 hours or up to two weeks.

2 Shake well before pouring into serving glasses. Serve with a sprinkle of cinnamon and decorate with a cinnamon stick.

Purple Boba Tea

¼ cup **sugar**

¼ cup **black tapioca pearls** (boba)

1 bag **black tea**

½ cup **whole milk**

2 tablespoons unsweetened **taro powder**

Ice cubes

Helpful Hint

The tapioca pearls (boba) are easily found online or in many Asian grocery stores. Be sure to read the back of the package to confirm boiling directions.

Bubble tea, or boba, is a Taiwanese invention from the 1980s. Typically a mixture of tea, milk, and ice, the defining element is the topping of little pearls of chewy tapioca starch (also called boba), which get sucked up via an extra-wide straw with every sip of the milky tea. There are a million variations in flavoring and topping, but arguably the G.O.A.T. of bubble teas is taro, made from the root vegetable. A purple hue plus a sweet, nutty flavor, makes every sip tea-riffic!

1 In a small saucepan, bring 1 cup of water and the sugar to a boil over high heat. Add the tapioca pearls and boil for 1 to 2 minutes, until the balls are swollen and floating. Remove from the heat and add the tea bag. Let steep for 2 minutes, then remove the tea bag. Cover the saucepan and let the tapioca pearls soak for 30 minutes.

2 In a cocktail shaker, combine the milk, taro powder, and ½ cup of ice cubes. Shake vigorously for about 30 seconds, until the taro powder is absorbed by the milk. Pour the flavored milk and the ice cubes into a large glass, then add the tea with the tapioca pearls. Stir to combine, then top off with more ice cubes before serving.

A

B

C

Agua Fresca with Chia

2 cups chopped **fresh honeydew melon**

1 **fresh cucumber**, peeled, cut in half, seeds removed, and roughly chopped

¾ cup **sugar**

¼ cup **chia seeds**

Helpful Hint

Chia seeds swell with a gelatin coating when soaked in liquid, sort of like a sponge expanding in water. Don't worry, they're perfectly safe (and delicious) to drink!

Agua fresca is a drink made from fruits, grains, or flowers blended with sugar and water. Popular across Mexico and Central America, and in Latin American communities in the United States, its common flavors include tamarind, horchata, hibiscus, or any ripe fruits. Here, we use a balance of honeydew and cucumber for a delicious but not-too-sweet result. Adding chia, a hyper-nutritious seed native to Mexico, ups the healthy factor while adding a fun texture from the gelatinous coating of the soaked seeds. It's the perfect drink for a hot day!

1 Add the melon, cucumber, and sugar to a blender along with 2 cups of cold water. Blend on high speed until completely smooth, 1 to 2 minutes. Set a fine-mesh strainer over a large bowl and pour the juice through the strainer. Use a wooden spoon to stir the pulp and release more liquid into the bowl. Pour the strained liquid into a large pitcher.

2 Place the pulp back in the blender and add 4 cups of cold water. Blend on high speed again to get a slurry, about 1 minute. Pour the slurry through the strainer into the bowl. Again, use a wooden spoon to stir the pulp and release more liquid into the bowl. Add the strained liquid to the pitcher and discard the pulp.

3 Stir the chia seeds into the pitcher liquid, cover the pitcher with plastic wrap, and refrigerate for at least 1 hour or up to 8 hours. Stir well before serving.

Homemade Ginger Ale

8 ounces **fresh ginger**, peeled and sliced

1 cup **sugar**

Ice cubes, for serving

Club soda or **seltzer water**, for serving

Ginger was used as a medicinal herb in Southeast Asian countries like the Philippines, Indonesia, and Malaysia. It traveled along the spice routes, was a hit with ancient Greeks, and spread far into Western Europe. In the 1850s, an Irish doctor, Thomas Joseph Cantrell, invented a dark and spicy brew of ginger ale, but it was John McLaughlin, a Canadian pharmacist, who in 1904 invented the pale dry (do those words sound familiar?) ginger ale we most commonly drink. This recipe for ginger ale not only makes your kitchen smell amazing as it simmers, but it also provides a jar of concentrated ginger syrup to enjoy all week.

1 In a medium saucepan, stir together the ginger and sugar. Cover and let sit for 30 minutes, until the ginger has begun to macerate.

2 Add 2 cups of water to the saucepan and bring to a boil over high heat. Cover, reduce the heat to low, and simmer for about 30 minutes, until the ginger is completely soft. Let cool completely, covered, about 2 hours.

3 Strain the ginger syrup through a fine-mesh strainer into a pint jar, discarding the ginger pieces. Cover and refrigerate until ready to serve or up to 1 week.

4 To serve the ginger ale, fill a highball glass with ice cubes. Pour the ginger syrup over the ice halfway up the glass and top with club soda.

Spiced (and Spiked) Apple Cider

Serves 8

FOR THE ICE RING

3 sprigs **fresh thyme**

½ **red apple,** cored and thinly sliced

½ cup frozen **cranberries**

FOR THE CIDER

½ cup **sugar**

1 (3-inch) piece **fresh orange peel**

1 (1-inch) piece **fresh ginger,** peeled and sliced

2 **star anise,** plus more as needed

2 **cinnamon sticks,** plus more as needed

1 quart **fresh apple cider**

1 (12-ounce) can **ginger beer**

½ cup **spiced rum** or **whisky**

Club soda or **seltzer water,** for serving

Frozen **cranberries,** for serving

Americans and apples had a rough start (see page 156), but we've *always* been a fan of apple cider. American colonists drank the cider daily because the available water was often contaminated, while the alcohol in the fermented cider made it the safer choice. (Even kids got to drink diluted cider!) The classic winter drink of mulled cider gets a makeover here with this perfectly spiced and lightly boozy punch bowl featuring a suspended ice ring. We used decorative herbs and fruit, but let your imagination run wild to create the best centerpiece ever!

1 Make the ice ring: Lay the thyme sprigs along the bottom of a 10-inch Bundt pan. Arrange the apple slices around the pan, then sprinkle in the cranberries. Fill the pan about one-third of the way with water, or until the apple slices are submerged. (Some cranberries will float.) Cover the pan with plastic wrap and freeze for 4 hours or up to 24 hours.

2 Make the cider: In a small saucepan, bring 1 cup of water and the sugar to a boil over high heat. Remove from the heat and add the orange peel, ginger, 2 star anise, and 2 cinnamon sticks. Cover and let cool completely, about 2 hours.

3 To a punch bowl, add the apple cider, ginger beer, and rum. Set a fine-mesh strainer over the bowl and pour the cooled syrup through it. Discard the orange peel, ginger, and spices. Remove the ice ring from the freezer. Turn upside down and place your hand beneath the center opening. Run the mold under warm water until the ice falls into your hand, then quickly transfer the ring to the punch bowl.

4 To serve, ladle the punch into glasses, top with some club soda, and garnish with additional star anise and cinnamon, and a few cranberries.

Caramel Coffee Frappe

Makes 1 drink

1 cup **ice cubes**

¼ cup **instant coffee granules**

½ cup **whole milk**, very cold

¼ cup **caramel sauce**, plus more
  for serving

Whipped cream,
  for serving

There's a certain coffee chain that sells a certain mashup of frappé and cappuccino. The popular drink is a blending of a Greek frappé (coffee, sugar, water, and milk, shaken until frothy), a New England frappe (a thick milkshake, pronounced "frap"), and an Italian cappuccino (espresso and foamed milk). Despite that complicated math, it's actually super simple to make at home and whole a lot faster than waiting in line. A powerful blender and a few ingredients are all it takes for an instant refresh!

1 Add the ice, coffee granules, milk, and caramel to a blender. Blend on high speed until fully combined, about 1 minute.

2 Pour the frappe into a chilled glass. Top with the whipped cream and a drizzle of caramel before serving.

Banana Cardamom Lassi

1 cup plain **full-fat yogurt** (see Note)

2 ripe **bananas**, peeled and chopped

1 tablespoon **sugar**

1 teaspoon **ground cardamom**

½ teaspoon **kosher salt**

½ teaspoon **freshly ground black pepper**

½ cup **ice water**

Lassi, a popular blended yogurt drink originating in northern India and the Punjab region of Pakistan, comes in many varieties. The ubiquitous one in America is the sweet and tangy mango lassi, but other popular varieties include salty (namkeen), buttery (makkhaniya), and even cannabis-infused (bhang). This banana lassi is kind of sweet, a little salty, and has a fragrant hint of cardamom. But most of all, it's cold, refreshing, and deeply satisfying.

1 Add the yogurt, bananas, sugar, cardamom, salt, pepper, and ice water to a blender. Blend on high speed until completely smooth, 30 seconds to 1 minute.

2 Pour into glasses and serve immediately.

Helpful Hint

Although thicker Greek yogurt is popular these days, go for the old school thinner, unstrained yogurt. It'll give the lassi a perfectly smooth and drinkable texture.

Acknowledgments

Author and Original Recipe Developer

Casey Elsass

Recipe Tester

Jacqueline Tris

Everyone at Tasty

Emily DePaula

Gwenaelle Le Cochennec

Parker Ortolani

Ines Pacheco

Eric Karp

Jessica Jean Jardine

Jordan Kenna

Pierce Abernathy

Katie Aubin

Marissa Buie

Betsy Carter

Matthew Johnson

Madhumita Kannan

Kiano Moju

Andrew Pollock

Alexander Roberts

Devin Rogerino

Karlee Rotoly

Hong Thaimee

Frank Tiu

Vaughn Vreeland

And the entire Tasty & BuzzFeed team

Everyone at Potter

Susan Roxborough

Robert Diaz

Jan Derevjanik

Mark McCauslin

Jen Wang

Stephanie Huntwork

Lydia O'Brien

Marysarah Quinn

Derek Gullino

Carole Berglie

Kelli Tokos

Merri Ann Morrell

Kate Tyler

Windy Dorresteyn

Andrea Portanova

Raquel Pelzel

Aaron Wehner

Francis Lam

Jill Flaxman

Styling and Photography

Lauren Volo

Monica Pierini

Maeve Sheridan

Christina Zhang

Krystal Rack

Aliyah Pair

Tsering Dolma

Index

Library of Congress Cataloging-in-Publication Data
is available.

ISBN 978-0-593-23345-0
Ebook ISBN 978-0-593-23346-7

Printed in China

Photographs by Lauren Volo
Book design by Jan Derevjanik
Cover design by Robert Diaz

10 9 8 7 6 5 4 3 2 1

First Edition

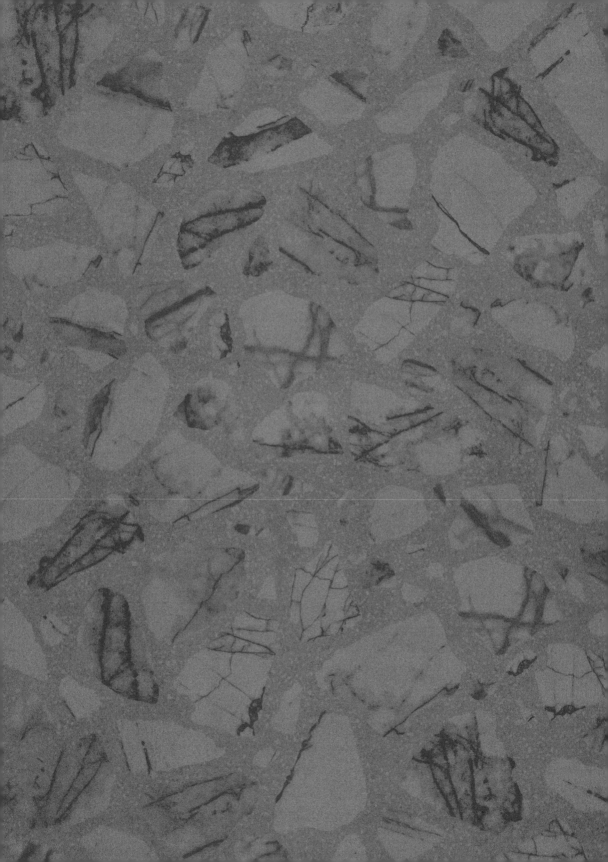